"The culture and health of an organization are built upon relationships and the ability for the leaders and team members to foster and sustain honest and supportive relationships. Roger Gerard provides both a theoretical and applied approach to the art of developing leaders and creating and sustaining actively engaged cultures. Roger's experience in organizational operations and learning and development, along with his passion for enhancing cultures by developing leaders, places him in a unique position as a thought leader and expert in assessing and enhancing organizational cultures. *Owning the Room* is a must read for any leader who desires to transform their organization's culture and performance to meet the needs of today and tomorrow."

—Candice Saunders, president and CEO Wellstar Health System

"This book should be required reading for all who are learning about leadership! The content, storytelling, and activities kept me engaged throughout the book. This hit home!

—Julie Brussow, CEO, Security Health Plan

"This work will touch the hearts and minds of all leaders who read it!"

—Andrew Cox, chief of staff to the CEO, WellStar Healthcare System

"A book focused on leading with mind, heart, and spirit to make extraordinary choices in a demanding world should always be welcomed. However, a thoughtful, practical, and thoroughly engaging work about the topic as the global Covid-19 crisis unfolds is truly a gift of impeccable timing. No organization and no leader escapes disruption. The only questions are how much and for how long? *Owning the Room* does not "admire the problem"—rather, it guides current and future leaders not only to lead change, but to become professionals prepared to lead *through* change, no matter how novel. In my experience, the best leaders 'own the room' by having one foot in the library and one foot in the street. On multiple occasions I have seen Dr. Gerard own the room as he masterfully leads organizations and groups through challenging times. All leaders will now benefit from his ability to bring both feet into *Owning the Room*."

—David A. Shore, PhD, author and former associate dean of Harvard University and former distinguished professor of innovation and change at Tianjin University of Finance and Economics (China)

"This book is terrific, a must-read leadership examination of confidence! The theme of mind, heart, and spirit will challenge all leaders on some level to improve their effectiveness. The content and format for each chapter, together with a section at the end for reflections and challenges provides the reader with a framework for a very personal, deep evaluation of their effectiveness. The emphasis on the leader's responsibility for the full continuum of their behaviors and the impact of these behaviors on the organization's performance is really key. The content is authentic, reflecting the author's years of executive and consulting work. The sections on change, culture, and working with others to achieve their full potential are so true and particularly resonated with me. Reading the book was an opportunity for me to reflect on my own leadership highs and lows. More highs than lows. But it was always the latter where deep painful learning occurred."

—Paul Macek, retired CEO

"This is truly an inspiring, powerful book! The way it is broken into three parts is wonderful... I loved this book, and can't wait to pass this gift on to so many others."

—Melissa Breen, chief of staff to the CEO, Marshfield Clinic Health System

OWNING
the
ROOM

 FriesenPress

Suite 300 - 990 Fort St
Victoria, BC, V8V 3K2
Canada

www.friesenpress.com

ISBN
978-1-5255-7543-3 (Hardcover)
978-1-5255-7544-0 (Paperback)
978-1-5255-7545-7 (eBook)

1. BUSINESS & ECONOMICS, LEADERSHIP

Distributed to the trade by The Ingram Book Company

Owning the Room

Leading with Mind, Heart and Spirit to Make
Extraordinary Choices in a Demanding World

Roger A. Gerard, PhD

TABLE OF CONTENTS

FOREWORD

I've worked closely with Roger Gerard across many years and with several organizations. What has always impressed me most about Roger's approach to leadership is his ability to strip away the superficial trappings—title, salary, and experience—and force leaders to dig deeper into their hearts and souls.

Roger understands that leadership is a pursuit fundamentally defined by human connection. He has taught me that leaders must put their hearts and souls into their work before others will follow.

As I write this, the medical community has been flipped upside down by COVID-19. Health-care leaders are being tested like never before, and leadership has never been more critical. I personally reflect on Roger's teachings and advice on a daily basis as I lead my executive team and our health system through this unprecedented crisis.

In the pages ahead, you'll find content that challenges you to define what truly matters to you as a leader. You'll find thought-provoking questions and useful exercises to hone your leadership toolkit. And you'll come away from this book with a new perspective and new ideas to become a more effective leader.

I have seen Roger Gerard in action, working with our board of directors at Marshfield Clinic Health System. He has a unique ability to make seasoned leaders reconsider long-held perspectives by challenging their traditional ways of thinking.

Simply put, if you want to be a better leader, and you want to improve leadership within your organization, this book is a must read.

—Susan Turney MD, CEO, Marshfield Clinic Health System

Mind, Heart, and Soul in the Middle of Chaos

"One of the major dilemmas we face… is simplistic thinking—
or the failure to think at all. It isn't just a problem, it is the problem."
—Peck, 1987, p.4

WARNING: This book may be hazardous to your current understanding of leadership, because leadership is not for amateurs. It is about creating extraordinary results. Acting on the principles within may cause unsettled responses in you and in those around you. Expect to be provoked and perhaps inspired toward new ways of practicing leadership.

As a leader, do you "own the room"? Are you an "extraordinary" leader? These questions could not be simpler, yet the fact that they need to be asked underscores the complexity inherent in them. In this book, I will explore these questions in depth by drawing on my more than forty-five years of leadership experience, both successes and mistakes, that have enriched my understanding of what master leadership is, and how it must be cultivated. In addition, I will offer perspective enriched by many others in my life who have demonstrated profound mastery of the leadership dynamic, as well as my own academic grounding, and the experiential grounding required by any leader who expects to get good at it. Leadership must be learned on the ground, by being a leader and doing the hard work of leading others. Frankly, it's the only way. But in this book, I can serve as a coach, perhaps a mentor, and a voice that has been there, done that, and is still learning forty-five years later.

I have three book collections in my office. One is spilling over with texts on rational management and lean and process improvement (including my own, *On the Mend*, co-written with my colleague, John Toussaint, MD). In this library, I have the analytic knowledge and approaches needed to supervise others, manage by objectives, map a value stream, conduct a kaizen event, build a reasonably competent problem statement A3, deploy strategy, remove waste, and even "5-S" the shelves of books and the rest of my office. This is all *"mind"* work, useful in problem-solving or goal alignment. But there seems to be a perverse sort of pride in thinking that our problems are so special that we need special, rational solutions (think 6-sigma, lean, ninety-day workouts, etc.) when it is possible that simpler, more creative solutions are often available. The second collection contains tomes on inspiring leadership, encouraging me to engage followership, be strategically savvy, cultivate shared vision and purpose, transform my organization, challenge the status quo, and inject creativity and innovation into my work and the work of others—all of it *"heart"* work, appealing to the emotional commitment to the work. The third collection is comprised of countless works of a *spiritual nature*, focused on finding core purpose, connecting with forces greater than self, meditating mindfully, mastering self, and living a value-driven life of "soul intention." The contrast between these three libraries (one rational, one emotional, one spiritual) couldn't be more pronounced.

Despite searching, I haven't found work integrating the three bodies of knowledge in a sensible, action-inspired way. And none, by themselves, foster a mindset of creating extraordinary results. Most efforts confuse the reader, with over-scholarly research or pathetically weak, single-minded platitudes. Those focused on rational leadership contain mostly tools, with a few pages dedicated to often trite leadership advice about getting the work done. But work is how we make a living, while heartfelt is how we create a life! Those focused on heart leadership offer little tangible advice or "how-tos" for advancing emotional leadership competency. Leaders are exhorted to "drive change through the culture," "engage the people," or "this must be led from the top"—all presented as axioms that defy argument, with little in the way of specifics about how any of this should be accomplished. Few focus on leadership as a spiritual enterprise, or on the workplace as a place for inspiration, purpose-finding, or play. Leaders are left with centuries-old, Taylor-esque belief systems, treating people as machines to be adjusted through force of will, despite knowing that extraordinary performance through will alone will not sustain (Benjamin Hardy, 2018). All of this suggests an abysmal failure to recognize the true dynamics of leadership.

Worse, some "experts" promote behaviors that can only be described as offensive, encouraging a "walk of shame" or other humiliating exercises designed to blame and embarrass people for their mistakes, inefficiency, and waste. At one business meeting, a respected "sensei" proudly described demanding that an executive stand in a chalk circle on a manufacturing plant floor for hours, until he "got it" (seeing waste). Others refer to those who do not understand improvement principles or who drag their feet in implementation as "cement heads," "laggards," and unengaged. This disrespectful, spiritually bankrupt behavior passing as wisdom is justified, usually half apologetically and with a wink, as the "only way to get through to people." As a leader who teaches leaders, I have come to expect all kinds of silliness in the leadership development field… promoted by fools, frauds, and self-proclaimed experts, many selling unproven products and services. Our world is full of "quick fixes" that seldom fix, and that often make things worse. Incredibly, many of these charlatans have no management experience themselves, coming from academia or other pursuits. Others, even those with experience, think that they can push the culture to change rapidly. But they are encouraging change too fast, with no respect for history or the culture within which they are working. Such nonsense has no place in any environment that claims "respect for people" as a fundamental premise. In this book, I will not defend any practices that deplete human spirit.

People generally do not come into leadership knowing how to lead. The result is that many organizations are

"In this book, I will not defend any practices that deplete human spirit."

being led by people who are masters in their professional disciplines, but amateurs as leaders. As a result, they are focusing on obligations over possibility, on the "must dos" rather than on the "can dos." Most of us need to be shown and taught how to lead. Ultimately, people who have mastered leadership are not trying to be masters. Rather, they have decided to create extraordinary results… all in! Mastery is a practice with no shortcuts, requiring mind, heart, and spirit. When you achieve it, you can "own the room."

Leadership is about "cultural alchemy," the forging of the base "metals" of the organization (people's mind, heart, and spirit) into the "gold" of extraordinary results. To achieve extraordinary results, you must make extraordinary choices, and often expose yourself to the heat of inspection and criticism as you make difficult decisions. This book is about fostering the *human* enterprise, describing how truly professional leaders go beyond rational problem-solving/decision-making or brute force to achieve extraordinary results, and bring more heart into the work, ultimately appealing to the human spirit in providing meaning and purpose. You will learn from the real experiences of others how to balance mind with heart and spirit to accomplish intentions, including detailed action steps you can take to get started. Reflecting *and acting on* the principles in this book offer insight that will enable true development as a high-performing master leader who gets things done. You can be the extraordinary leader that you aspire to be!

Why this book now?

Look around! We live in a world of constant change, often bordering on chaos. Everything is moving faster than ever, and technology tests every leader's ability to keep up. It often seems that the technology is managing us, rather than the other way around. Work is increasingly depersonalized, with people showing clear signs of alienation through increasing absenteeism, substance abuse, cynicism, litigation, and half-hearted contribution to daily work. Leaders need a fully integrated approach that marries rational intention, heart, and spirit if they are to navigate effectively. This book is divided into three parts, and pursues three purposes: 1) *Leadership Action as Intention*: to lay a thoughtful foundation for both practiced and new leaders who are learning leadership on the job; 2) *Making it Happen—Putting Foundations to Work*: to detail the actions necessary to master leadership and address some of the misconceptions that exist about what leadership is and is not; 3) *Deepening the Learning*: to encourage the continued learning of leadership through guided thought, and *practice through action and experimentation.*

This is not an academic thesis, crammed with data and research findings to be read only by other academics. Such books languish, seldom making any difference in anyone's life. I am writing about what is possible, what is practical, from lessons that come from my experience and the experience of others in their leadership practice in the environment of continual change and obsessive customer focus. There is no real lesson plan for learning to lead, except to lead. The heat of experience forges leadership excellence, and everything else is an unnecessary distraction. This book is a practitioner's guide to learning by leading, building wisdom through action and experience. There is not enough space in a book to cover all of what matters most in leadership. I will focus here on those things that have resonated as most effective in my career as both a leader and a consultant to many leaders. You, the reader, picked this book up for your own reasons, and this suggests that you may be ready to learn and grow as a leader. Take the time to read, reflect, and then act. You owe it to yourself and will learn much, though I will also promise that the "heat" will sometimes be uncomfortable.

"Take the time to read, reflect and then act."

Premises underlying this work

My own experiential learning, assumptions, and limitations are embedded in this work. What I have found is that one ingredient absent in much of leadership today is "leadership intelligence," which I define as the wise integration of the rational, emotional, and spiritual realities of life. It is fair to expose some of my own experiential learning, so the reader knows my context. Each premise that follows is grounded in long practice and experience as a manager, an executive, a teacher, and a consultant to many who have mastered leadership. Many of these premises could be expanded into an in-depth study for those so inclined, but I am *not*, and leave detailed research to others. All of these premises will be touched on in the following chapters, and serve as the foundational "thought framework" for the approaches this work details. Here they are:

> » *Heroic problem-solving is not leadership*: society has deified leadership as the ultimate problem-solvers and heroic saviors, worshiping those deities at the altar of data and information. This is misleading and such leaders are most often destructive, resulting in predictable failure, blaming, and retribution, followed by cynicism and fear. The leader's primary role is neither problem-solving nor heroism (Bradford & Cohen, 1998), as neither grows the organization toward its future. Such leader behavior only leads to the discovery of more problems, reinforces the "need" for more problem-solvers, and, in the long-term, degrades performance. You get what you focus on. Extraordinary leaders build communities of practice organized around purpose and values, create an environment of interpersonal autonomy and accountability, and foster continual learning. They ask new questions, create new possibilities, and leave problem-solving to the staff doing the daily work.

> » *Teamwork and participation are never permission to abdicate leader responsibility*: engaging people in the decisions that affect them has been a staple of leadership thinking for decades. But it often goes too far. Some decisions belong to leadership. It is important to be clear

about when participation is appropriate and when it is not. This will be treated fully in Chapter 11.

» *Empathy will never fix bullies or self-appointed victims, and life is full of them:* Anxiety and fear are common in the workplace, often exacerbated by legitimate distrust of leadership (and sometimes colleagues). Friedman (*Failure of Nerve,* 2007) teaches us that autocratic and mechanistic approaches to leadership breed impersonalization and alienation. The result is a culture that permits bullying and places a high value on victimization, encouraging misplaced empathy for the "victims." In addiction counseling, this is called "enabling behavior." Today, there is no time for those who fail to take personal accountability for their work. Empathy and autocracy are both forms of control that deepen dependency, encouraging heroic behavior and fostering more bullying, blaming, and victim behaviors when things fail. In such an environment, engagement will not sustain.

» *Metrics are overused, and usually abused:* People do their best work when they understand expectations and have the freedom to operate within their knowledge and skill. Metrics are *necessary* for this to occur. But metrics, combined with a societal addiction to "more and faster," are often taken too far, drowning people under a typhoon of data, encouraging more nuanced forms of bullying, and dooming us to react in low-value, uncaring way. In addition, we tend to believe that what we can measure is all that there is—a belief that is far from truth. Extraordinary leaders focus on the critical few metrics and forget the rest, understanding that "directionally correct" is more important than perfection in most instances, and that at times, human factors are more important than the daily work being done.

» *Certainty is a myth:* Everything is temporary. The obsessive quest for security, consistency, and standardization leads to ever-increasing, spirit-depleting controlling behaviors, and even more anxiety and fear. Policies, rules, and overly standardized processes suck the energy and joy out of daily work in profoundly deadening ways—no heart, no spirit. Today, more and better decisions can be executed faster only when people are free of unnecessary rules (Lakhiani, 2018).

» *You cannot change the culture by edict:* a question often asked is: "How exactly do I change the culture?" Simply, you can't! (Or perhaps better stated, you shouldn't!) The culture does not easily change, but rather lives in the human relationships of the organization, and emerges in the conversations and relationships. Cultural change is evolutionary, an adaptive process, a result of changing our conversations and relationships. If you inherit a chaotic culture, it sometimes may be necessary to "use a hammer" to set new expectations, but you must know when to put the hammer down!

I've heard leaders complain that the world is not organized for them to be successful. One recent executive tirade was to the point:

> *"Why aren't people more engaged? I told them what needed to be done. Why didn't it happen? Why do I have to do everything? How do I get buy-in from my staff? No one seems to care around here! I am expected to increase productivity, reduce costs, and keep my people happy!!! What are they thinking?! Nobody cares about loyalty anymore. They just don't get it. I have to create a 'burning platform' to get people moving! It seems like everyone is delegating up to me! What is all of this learned helplessness about!?"*

Excuse me, but who taught them to be helpless? Such complaints, and the frustrated tone of voice, betray leaders who believe they have no power, an adult form of a two-year-old's temper tantrum. It also reveals a workplace with strong intention, but devoid of heart and spirit. My response: I reject that reality, and prefer to substitute my own. Get a grip! The world is *not* organized for your needs! The leader must rise to the daily challenges that occur. Be a leader, or remove yourself from leadership. It is time to be professional!

> » Intention is never about "kinda" wanting something. "Kinda" intention leads to "kinda" results. When you bring people together without clear purpose, you are just annoying them! Leaders declare absolute intention.

"You cannot change the culture by edict."

This book is an action book that offers approaches to foster a healthier sense of authentic power and accountability, and perhaps a bit of wisdom along the way. It includes provocative, challenging ideas useful in making change, while honoring principles "hard-wired" into the human condition. Change, for many leaders, has been an intellectual idea, rather than personal: "Change is needed, *and you* better get started!" Those days are over. It is leadership that must change. Emphasis here is on the "what and the how" of leadership. Those who want to know "why" can read the many texts cited in the "Readings" section of the appendix. They are excellent. What is presented here is practical and actionable right now. After each chapter, you are asked to "go and see, go and do." That is where the real learning takes place, where the raw materials of working life are melted and transformed into the "gold" of extraordinary performance.

While some things can be learned effectively in a textbook, I know from experience that leadership is not one of them. To learn leadership, one must lead. No book can make you a better leader. Action is required for impact. Impact is required for relevance. When you go and see, you often discover things you really did not know that are happening in your place of work. Take the challenge to go and see, to truly understand the work and the people who are doing it, and what practical things must be done to make it all effective! Use the tools within, however they are helpful, but do not be enslaved by them. It is not my intent to add more tasks to an already over-full task list, but to provoke new thinking and new approaches to the work you are already doing. In reading this, don't take everything offered as necessary or important. Rather, take what is meaningful, and discard the rest. Don't obsess over how change will occur. Rather, focus on what you are thinking and doing, right now. The first and most important change is the change within.

I know this sounds ambitious, but if you learn the foundational principles in this leadership book, you may never need another. Consider this book as a set of passages—doorways, if you will—to shared experience and extraordinary results. It is more than a collection of words and stories. Rather, view this as a way of connecting with a larger body of wisdom. To some, the contents that follow might seem inconsistent, even contradictory. Life is not linear, not everything is a problem to be solved, and sometimes emotional problems arise that defy rational, logical solutions. Pay attention. In those moments, you can most powerfully engage the heart and spirit, and earn your right to lead. This book, if truth be told, is not my book, but the accumulation of wisdom and experience of many exceptional people who have gone before us. I have been their student. I have deliberately chosen to use stories in this book from my own experience as leader, and as a coach to leaders. This is personal to me, and teaching authentic leadership requires that I write from authentic experience, rather than from created case studies. Perhaps reading the stories throughout this book will encourage you to think about your own leadership, and the extraordinary results in your work. They are all true, though names and circumstances have been altered out of respect. With that, I take full responsibility for everything here. Like most books of this type, it is an integration of my experience, my studies and my informed opinions. It is your choice to agree or not and to act or not... but I encourage you to consider what you read with a willingness to have your position influenced. Read, reflect, go and see, and then practice—not only with your head but with your heart and spirit! Take action!

PART 1:

Extraordinary Leadership Requires Acting on Knowledge and Awareness

---

"Awareness means to open your eyes to see the truth…"
(Ruiz, p. 27)

Knowledge is not truth, but merely what is known. And often what we "know" is later found to be untrue! No one has absolute truth. What I know may be very different from what you know. Perspectives vary, meaning that no one is ever actually "right" about much. In this first part, the focus is on cultivating knowledge and awareness, beginning with an understanding of why you have entered leadership, and the personal nature of mastered leadership. Extraordinary leaders do not live ordinary lives. Rather, they create intention offering new opportunities, new paths, new relationships, and new results for themselves and, equally important, for others. Do you know your intentions? Are you acting to realize them? Are you focused and inspired? Do those who follow you feel your care for them (your "heart"), and do you make sure they have the necessary resources to accomplish their purpose? Are they inspired ("in spirit")? How do you know? Does your work feed people's spirit, as a source of meaning? Such questions do not get much "face time" in a world obsessed with problem-solving and quick fixes. Yet they are at the heart of leadership mastery.

Much is available to help leaders succeed: teachers and mentors, published research, and a community of others ready to share what they know. Every experience can be a moment of growth. Your first and most important step is realizing that you must learn what is required to be an extraordinary, high-performing, professional leader.

CHAPTER 1

I Am a Leader...
What Have I Gotten
Myself Into?!

"We speak endlessly, both in the public conversation and privately, about the rise and fall of leaders. The agenda this sustains is that leaders are cause and all others are effect. That all that counts is what leaders do."
—Block, 2009, Pp. 40-41

KEY POINTS SUMMARY

» Leadership is a practice improved by experience, much like medicine, law, and other practice-based professions.

» Extraordinary leaders change things in big ways, acting on possibility and vision.

» There are three action-based practices for effective leadership mastery, and specific steps to effective practice. Leaders must: 1) create clear and focused intention, 2) nurture engagement by demonstrating heartfelt care, and 3) connect work to inspiring meaning and purpose.

» Leadership occurs in a complex, sometimes counter-intuitive, changing environment, requiring that leaders challenge their own assumptions and respectfully change themselves before working to change others. Such challenge offers the best prospects for extraordinary success.

It happened in early 1990. I settled down, at home in my chair with a fire in the fireplace, my intent to relax, read the newspaper, and perhaps doze a bit. The blue waters of Lake Michigan brightened my living room window, the sun sparkling on a fresh snow, and the day felt good. But as I opened my paper, I suddenly felt a chill. There, staring back, was a head shot of me, with a quarter-page spread detailing my background and announcing my recent promotion to vice president of the largest enterprise in our northern Michigan community. As the oldest child of a blue-collar family, the idea that this 1960s establishment protester would someday be an executive was not on anyone's written plan. Yet there it was. Strangely, I felt that the writer was describing somebody else, and that I was an imposter. What had I just gotten myself into? I later learned that my reaction was not unusual. Change inevitably brings each of us to decision turning points, requiring that we redefine who we are and what we are doing, creating obstacles to overcome and new goals to achieve. Anxiety, ambiguity, and uneasiness with change are natural human feelings, not symptoms that something is wrong. With good mentors in my life, over time I did accept that I had become an executive (for better or for worse). One mentor in particular was direct. "Welcome" he said, "to what will be the most difficult job in your life. Make sure you love it!" After several decades, I know that he was right. Though difficult, I have loved it. Read on...

What do those who have mastered leadership practice do?

This first chapter defines three action-based leadership practices for leading intentionally. These practices—employing the mind, heart and spirit to accomplish intention—organize this book. But first, consider leadership in contrast to the manager function. Leaders and managers are different, and the differences are not minor. To the manager, work life is a series of problems to be solved and tasks to be completed. To the leader, work life is adventure, opportunities to be taken, and possibility to be chased. At the management level, we bring knowledge and skills—hiring, scheduling, finance, problem-solving, etc. What happens in most effective organizations is simply good management, stabilizing things, creating predictability through standardized behaviors and processes, setting policy, hiring and deploying staff, attending to budgets and production, and improving performance through process changes, all marvelous, value-adding management activities. But these actions are management, not leadership.

At the leadership level, in addition to management skills, we bring growth and change through wisdom, vision, compassion, courage, and intention. Leadership is a practice requiring that you question the present and craft the future—and do it all with certainty that your plans will always change. Leaders change things and act on new possibilities, new vision, and new energies. While managers use data and reason to drive decision-making and problem-solving, leaders must often rely on intuition and inspiration in the face of imperfect data. While managers work to minimize risk and amplify results, leaders use calculated risk as a source of energy and focus. Managers bring a level of rational pragmatism to the work, while leaders bring a measure of emotional energy and opportunism. In a very real way, it is the leader's job to disturb the peace while demonstrating heart and ensuring that those doing the work find meaning that feeds their spirit. If you want extraordinary performance, it is not enough to be "realistic" or "reasonable," to do the expected or to be "normal." You must be willing to be different, extraordinarily different. Today, more than ever, society needs bold, courageous, and perhaps *unreasonable* leaders willing to act in an environment of constant change, people who can exercise intuition and judgment while taking risks to make things better. Such intentional leaders are driven by passion and fulfilled by extraordinary results.

"If you want extraordinary performance… you must be willing to be different, extraordinarily different."

Where are all of the great leaders?

Recruiting professionals know that finding and keeping great leaders is difficult and expensive. In 2015, the average fee for executive search was around $140,000 (Executive.com). And once hired, there are on-boarding and orientation costs, first-year development costs, and the costs associated with the vacancy while the position is unfilled. Only a small number aspire to take full leader responsibility with accountability, and to do the difficult things that improve business performance while inspiring those around them. Those few still struggle with the challenges. The 2015 CEO Success Study by PwC's Strategy& reports that CEO turnover rates were roughly 17 percent per year globally, a rate that has been climbing over time (https://www.strategyand.pwc.com/ceosuccess). Manager turnover is not far behind. Leadership is demanding work, a fact that those who are not leaders seldom fully understand or appreciate.

Authentic leadership is an ensemble of three foundational practices

Like medicine, law and education, leadership is a professional practice, learned over time through experience. Leadership integrates three different human practices in one motion: employing rationality to define and promote intention (mind), connecting emotionally (heart), and inspiring purpose (spirit). Each practice is a mix of behaviors occurring simultaneously with the other practices, rather than independently. Like the conductor of an orchestra who practices first with the string instruments then with percussion and then with the horn section, the leader can independently study each of the foundational leader practices before bringing them together in full orchestration. Only then can you begin to master leadership practice as a full discipline. Mastery will be measured over months or even years, and it will require rigor, compassion, and self-motivation.

Practice 1: *Employing Mindful Intention (cultivating mind)—Connecting Rationally:* Consider the best leaders in your life. Odds are that they were great listeners who offered profound wisdom and vision, who knew their stuff and what they had to do to be successful. They also knew and watched the metrics of the business. These leaders were aware of potential problems and risks, and knew what to do when things did not go as planned. They were knowledgeable, aware, rational, and intentional.

Intentional leaders are authentic, focused on the purposes of the business, devoid of blatant self-interest. They focus first on the needs of the customer and on the specific requirements of the products and services for that customer. However, forming rational intention is insufficient by itself. Effective leaders also know how to manage and promote *attention* on their intention, and this is where what I call "Heart Intention" enters.

"Effective leaders know how to promote attention on their intention!"

Practice 2: *Cultivating Heart Intention (Care)— Connecting Emotionally:* Leadership would be simple if it were merely a process devoid of human emotion and care for others. But it would also be less meaningful, less human. Emotion moves people, and the lack of it unsettles people. Most behavior is motivated by either love or fear, and fear is never a great platform for healthy, long-term engagement in the work. As a current executive colleague, Jerard Jensen (EVP and general counsel for Marshfield Clinic Health System) recently told me, "Fear is a strong motivator, but it is corrosive to the spirit and will ultimately become a self-fulfilling prophecy."

Engaging others is both a skill and an art, much like love. It begins with noticing results, strengths, talent, and, most importantly, humanity. The heart-intentional leader monitors and manages flow, troubleshoots and firefights, and keeps everyone focused on the work requirements until the job is done, *while paying close attention to the emotional content of the work.* Work is emotional. As intention forms, *authentic* leaders ensure that competencies and skills are there to deliver products and services, doing so in a manner that projects interest in and care for the people doing the work. This requires orchestrating complex factors, including: joining different disciplines to work in partnership; respecting distinct personalities among employees; attending to resource issues with full attention to financials, inventory, and flow; valuing cultural history and experience; and staying aware of changing circumstances, environmental conditions, and customer expectations. Care for the people doing the actual work of the organization means treating them respectfully as experts and true assets. Extraordinary leaders pay attention to the little things. They know that little things matter in big ways for most people: praise for a task well done, a note of appreciation, friendly inquiries about family, and so on. Leadership is about breaking through, moving from follower to creator, from complier to initiator, while appealing to those doing the day-to-day work from the heart. Heartfelt care opens the path to doing inspiring work for higher purpose.

Practice 3: *Cultivating Spirit Intention (Inspiration—Connecting to Purpose):* The intentional leader knows that people can become distracted and bored and helps them find purpose in work done well. Not only can workers engage in immediate tasks and duties, but also in the higher purposes of the organization, service to customers, solving big problems, and growing themselves professionally. True leadership is less about control and more about inspiring others to their own greatness. Extraordinary leaders will demonstrate such purpose first, along with the ability to learn, and then cultivate such learning on the part of everyone else to enable accomplishment of those higher purposes. Old competencies will obsolesce, allowing the reinvention of capabilities for all. When leaders master learning as a competency, they are managing the toughest challenge—themselves, and their own growth. And they are affecting the higher purposes of the organization in their own willingness to grow and change. This is inspiring to most.

In his book *Return on Character*, Fred Kiel describes the differences between what he calls "self-focused" and "virtuous" CEOs. (Kiel, 2015, pp. 22 &23) As a result of his research, he defines self-focused leaders as people who tend to focus on their own success and welfare, while the virtuous leaders focus on the success and welfare of the people doing the daily work and the business itself. He found that this signifi-cant initial driver sets the stage for significant differences in results, with the virtuous leaders excelling on almost every metric. This is about character!

Leadership is often counter-intuitive— challenge your assumptions!

Consider Jason's story. Jason was a manager/leader pro-moted from a technical professional role who, like many, believed that he must be able to do all that his staff does even better, so that he could help them out when they could not keep up. Unfortunately, because he was constantly helping his staff, his own work suffered, and his leadership was ineffective, causing his boss to be concerned about Jason's performance. This raised Jason's anxiety, driving him to even more "helping" behavior, a negative spiral in which he was creating results exactly opposite to what he intended. Ultimately, Jason, in frus-tration, reported that "everyone seems to be delegating up to me!" Clearly, this is not how delegation is supposed to work, and Jason was failing!

A basic problem for many amateur leaders is that they tend to believe as Jason did. Task expertise and "helping out staff" seem to be intuitive "common sense" approaches but are, in reality, a symptom of ego-centered ambition. Not only is the leader not helping, the leader is harming the organization, and the people involved, by robbing them of the opportunity to learn and grow from their own experience, while positioning himself as a "hero" manager, swooping in to save the day. Distress is a result of such ambition, not engagement. When ambition is self-serving, it will lead to anxiety, competitive behaviors, even

"True leadership is less about control and more about inspiring others to their own greatness."

9

anger and depression. Authentic ambition should focus instead on serving the more profound learning needs of others. Jason has a higher road available, albeit a more challenging one. Some of our most important drivers are a sense of ownership, accomplishment, and control over one's destiny. The solution: Contrary to his belief, Jason needed to separate himself from the staff work and start doing *his job*—that is, *being a leader*—defining the intentions, leading the team with heart, and not doing the team's work for them but insisting that the team experience meaning through accepting difficult challenges and learning how to do things themselves.

To move from doer to leader, one must give up old patterns, expectations, and relationships, a difficult challenge that often feels somehow wrong. Too often, leaders believe that a title, along with requisite salary, perks, and benefits, confers leader authority and power, and that, with the right tool in the right situation at the right time, they will have "arrived" as a competent leader. In Jason's case, he thought that by being able to do his staff's work "in order to help them," he was demonstrating leadership when, in fact, he was failing to build their competencies, and not doing his job!

The expectations and assumptions that we bring into leadership, fostered by media stereotyping and past experiences, are often unreasonable. Here is the reality:

» Leadership is not merely *common sense*. Anyone rationalizing decisions or behavior as "common sense" is likely a fraud! What you view as common sense might rationally be viewed by others as stupidity. We might think that the ceremonies of a religious faith are quite irrational, yet believe that studying monkeys in a cage to understand human behavior is somehow rational! Intentional leadership requires awareness beyond our own experience and knowledge, even about things that seem strange or unusual.

» If you are an executive or manager and doing the work that others were hired to do, you are doing someone else's job, and not your own job! Remember Jason's story!

» Getting things done will not be easier once you are the leader! You will work hard and long. Stay focused on intention!

» Your being a leader does not mean that people will want to follow you. It is likely that, *because you are the leader*, some will *not* want to follow. Your job is to win their confidence. That requires that you care about them, and demonstrate "heart."

» Amateur leaders promoted from "within" often claim that they can still remain friends with those former colleagues who are now on their staff. Your staff will not, and cannot, be "your friends," nor can you be theirs, no matter what the history has been. Being friendly is necessary, and you must lead with kindness. That is the meaning of "heart." Just recognize that today you have the power to terminate that friend's employment—and might have to someday. Everyone else knows this and so should you. It is time to get professional!

» Solving problems is not as easy as you might have thought it would be before you were a leader, and may not be the most important work of extraordinary leaders. Most problems that reach leaders are complex, requiring relational and navigational work to bring people together on common solutions. It is time to forget being the source of "right" answers and solutions. Focus instead on the desires that bring us energy, connection with one another, and engagement in ways that bring about better solutions. You can't flow-chart that! It happens though emotional connection, coming from the heart.

» Leaders are not born as leaders. Most have learned leadership from their experience, most notably from their failures—and so will you. This is humbling and challenging to the spirit. Just ask those in leadership positions… they'll tell you.

» Being a leader does not offer shelter from stress, anxiety, or fear. Far from it, those things might increase. You must be centered in spirit, in values based on experience, and you must utilize stress as the important tool it is, a signal that something needs to change.

» Past experience has not fully prepared you for today's leadership... you are not a finished product, even if this is your second or third leadership job. As in other endeavors, past performance is not necessarily the best indicator of future success. Continued learning is central to mastering effective and extraordinary leadership practice.

Things change—no kidding!

When I took my first supervisory leadership position, there was no internet, I typed on an IBM Selectric typewriter that replaced my old, black Smith-Corona, dictated copy into a Lanier belt recorder for transcription, and knew that a phone was not something I could put in my pocket! "App" was not a word, and my GPS was a paper map in my glove box. Tweeting was something that birds and whistles did. Clearly, things have changed—the leader must keep up! Our world is obsolescing our knowledge, skills, tools, and competencies every day. The idea that we can plan years into the future is naïve at best, and at worst, expensively risky. Real life always takes place in the middle of our best plans! (Think about the fall of Kodak with all of their film-based investments and the rise of digital photography in the space of a few short years! I love my Canon digital cameras!) Most plans fail in time, and when they do, your leadership begins.

When interviewing candidates for first-time leadership positions, a typical inquiry is whether they feel "up for the challenges" of the job, and why. The usual response is rapid: "Yes, I am up to the challenge, and my experience has prepared me!" Of course, the candidates are selling themselves, as they should. Almost without exception, however, the new leader will later proclaim, "I heard what you said about leadership being different, but I didn't really understand. This has been a difficult change for me." The work is daunting, their experience did not prepare them, and by now, they have likely experienced failure and self-doubt. Scott Peck calls this doubt "the beginning of wisdom." (Peck p. 46) Today's leader must learn new tasks, new relationships, new perspectives, new patterns and new accountabilities every day… demanding work, for which you can never fully prepare.

There are two ways to lead in a constantly changing world: focus on staying safe and secure solving daily problems, or focus on creating something entirely new. One is self-imprisonment, the other is freedom. Will you choose risk to achieve greatness? Or will you choose to be "realistic"? How will you change the conversation from identifying, parsing, and solving problems to declaring mindful intention, heart, and inspiration? This shift is the foundation of the extraordinary leader's power. The less time spent in creating and inspiring vision and intention, the more people are left to be reactive to their own desires and the desires of others, without real focus on the intentions of the organization. Too often, we are focused on the "how" of life without sufficient focus on the "what" of life. We forget our purpose and intentions as we obsess on our tasks. Failure to provide clear intention leaves that space open to old habits and patterns. As you learn the language of intentional leadership, prepare for a role requiring courage, focus, and a compassionate care for others. Getting focused means that you must decide that your goals are more important than the next "bright, shiny object."

"Getting focused means that you must decide that your goals are more important than the next 'bright shiny object.'"

What if there was a different purpose for leaders?

What if the purpose of leadership is to have everyone succeed in living life, doing those things necessary for both individual and organizational success? Today's "more and faster" culture has become fully fixed on the goals (read: financial, productivity, production) of the organization, with an expectation that individuals align their own goals and interests around them. It seems that the higher purposes of work in providing individual purpose and meaning has been forgotten. In one client business, a favorite theme of the domineering CEO was expressed as a harsh question, repeated countless times in the course of a day: "You get paid, don't you? Just get it done!" This CEO's workplace lacked heart and was not an inspiring place. Everyone dreaded his visits. When the purpose of leadership is to measure, monitor, pressure, and control, and to dwell primarily on the financials and other business metrics without regard for people, success for a few might be possible, but not likely, and it won't sustain over time. As one employee in this same company wrote in his employee survey, "It doesn't excite me to work my ass off, so that the company can save a buck for the idiot CEO! I'm here for the customer, and I love the work that I do. I *tolerate* our boss!" Leaders must be more heartfelt and inspiring than that! Leadership mastery is less about the accomplishment of daily work, and more about creating and affirming the connections between us. Are we inspiring people to make a living? Or to make a life of meaning?

What a good leader looks like … an evolving story!

Much research has been done in the last 100+ years to learn what sets apart highly effective leaders and managers. Researchers, beginning with Frederick Taylor (Scientific Leadership), Elton Mayo (Hawthorne studies), Abraham Maslow (Hierarchy of Needs), McGregor and Hertzberg (Theory X/Y, satisfiers/hygiene factors), and Blake & Mouton (grid theory) have all fed our knowledge about the leadership behavior that gets optimal organizational performance. Much of this is recounted in Blanchard and Hershey's book, *Management and Organizational Behavior: Utilizing Human Resources* (1988), and in the original research abstracts in *Models for Management: The Structure of Competence,* edited by John Shtogren (1980). The premise has been that, if employees could be motivated more effectively, better outcomes would occur. That premise is still alive. *Training Magazine* (July/ August 2013) features *four* articles on motivating employees "to achieve the next level," all of them placing the burden of creating motivation on the manager/leader/trainer. More recent focus has been on getting people "engaged," as if that is something leaders do to employees!

Intelligent leadership requires that we be wary of flimsy thinking, superficial ideas, formulaic solutions, and reactive fads and trends. Digging deeper into the research surfaces an annoying assumption: that people will be unmotivated/unengaged unless the boss motivates/engages them. Therefore, the people are the problem, and it is therefore leadership's job to solve the problem (i.e., to fix the people). Today, this line of thinking is evident in our countless policies, rules, disciplinary processes, incentives, cheerleading activities, labor contracts, and other controlling mechanisms, little of which creates motivated people. No one joins an organization to be "fixed" by someone else. We seem much more adept at understanding rules than communities, specific problems than systemic phenomena, and rational process than the entire rational/emotional/spiritual human presence. Many leaders I've known overvalue the financial and output metrics of the organization, and undervalue the processes for cultivating caring purpose and meaning in the work. As organizations navigate the increasingly turbulent processes of human performance, there is available more current knowledge for understanding the human motivational processes at work, and of the practices that form great leaders (Bennis, Nanus, Block, Friedman, Bridges, Isaacs, Nepo, and many others).

The rest of this book will detail three extraordinary leader practices (mind, heart, and spirit), and define what is required to master authentic, intentional leadership. Before you continue, consider the following two steps to beginning your leadership journey.

"No one joins an organization to be 'fixed' by someone else."

Two Steps to Get Started

Step 1—Reflections and Journal: To begin your journey as a developing intentional leader, take time to reflect on these questions, and journal your answers:

» Describe three "ideal" and three "ineffective" leaders from your experience. List what makes them ideal or ineffective.

» What are your reflections about leadership and your approach? What has been your journey into leadership and what have you learned? What is working? What is not working? Why have you chosen the leadership role? Take a few minutes and write the story of your growth into leadership. What do the events mean to you?

» What three intentions do you have for your organization, department, or division? What is the vision? Write it down!

Step 2—Actions: As an intentional leader, it is important for you to be clear about who you are, and what you are prepared to promise. More specifically, it is necessary and beneficial to declare your intentions, and your commitment to those on your team. Likewise, it is important for you to know theirs, so that you can help them achieve their goals and dreams. This step is an action step, designed to cause you to declare and act on your intentions, moving you forward, and to seek out an understanding of the intentions of others. Take this challenge and journal your learning when you have finished.

» Schedule a conversation with three trusted staff about what you see in your current situation, potential outcomes, your intentions, and about their opportunities. Make sure everyone has a chance to speak openly, without fear, about their perspectives. Find out their goals and dreams, and consider how they can further your own intentions. Do not interrupt, challenge, or criticize their intentions in any way. Just listen and take note.

» Make promises to your team members that you will help them. And ask for promises in return. Plan specific actions going forward, with clarity of responsibility.

» If there are relational issues between you and your staff, open conversations to begin resolving them. Invite feedback and reflect on your own role in creating those issues.

» Define three "first step" actions that further your intentions, and those of your staff.

» Go and see! Behind the scenes, take time to be with them, to understand their work, and to ensure that team members have what they need to experience success, and to learn from failure. Follow through on your plans, no excuses!

Pleasant reading and know that your journey has begun. You are taking on what will be the most difficult job of your career. Make sure that you know, when done, what you've gotten yourself into. Make sure you love it! And *learn by doing!*

CHAPTER 2

Acting on Mindful Intention

*"Leadership is the lifting of a man's vision to higher sights,
the raising of a man's performance to a higher standard, the building
of a man's personality beyond its normal limitation."*
—Drucker, 1973, p. 463

KEY POINTS SUMMARY

» You must know your intentions, communicate them, involve
others in them, and inspire others toward them. Why are
you here?

» Panaceas masquerading as solutions do not work! Likewise,
technique masquerading as leadership will fail!

» Know the intentions of those around you, and align those
intentions with your intentions. Do you know what others want
in their work?

» Be prepared to modify or even change your intentions based on
feedback from others.

» The solutions are not "out there." They are within.

With forgiveness to the late Dr. Drucker for his gender-specific language, the central premise still stands. What is your vision? Are your intentions clear and aligned with those around you? I am starting here because in our nine-to-five mentality, rational "mind work" is a given, and it is important. History is clear. Our best accomplishments emerge from the desire to make the world a better place, and then acting on that desire. To do that, intentional leaders must first have a clear vision. Leading is more about helping people understand and connecting them to intention than it is about solving problems or overcoming obstacles. Leaders get to choose: we can focus our purpose and intention on serving the needs of others, or we can be prisoners of our own ego, craving more and more without ever being satisfied with what we have. We usually discover our intentions by learning from others, experimentation, and reflecting over time. At first, those intentions may not be shared by others. Great ideas only become reality when people come together in mindful conversation about what matters most, so conversation, a lot of it, is necessary. This chapter describes that conversation, and what is required to create aligned intentions. Much of what is in this chapter is the practice of mind, focusing in on the rational, thinking part of the human experience. Leaders must use thoughtful processes and help others understand the reasoning behind intention. But first, a word of caution: rational thought is seldom sufficient! Heart and spirit work are equally important, and we will deal with them in later chapters.

"Let's set up a kiosk!"

Sometimes, amateur leaders fail to have the "intention" conversation. A client medical practice decided to install a new computerized records system to replace the current outdated system. The goals were improved efficiency, lower costs, and better-quality data faster—all admirable goals for the practice owners. The consultants, in a self-described "stroke of brilliance," placed a computer kiosk in the basement of the practice for use in training of staff during "off-hours, when they were not busy." They reasoned that such "off time" could be used to learn how to apply this new system to their day-to-day work without affecting the daily work. However, the computer kiosk went unused for weeks, and none of the staff learned how to use the new system. What could/should have been anticipated during what the consultants had labeled "off-hours," is that staff had other things to do, like record completion on the old system, lunch, break time, and finishing at the end of their shift to go home and make dinner for the family. There was little leadership understanding of the staff work patterns, and their entire implementation of the new system was deeply flawed. Lesson: if intention is anchored in flawed understandings, it will not be realized. Central to this failed initiative was the erroneous idea, stated by the physician leader, that employees, for some reason unknown, should "think like owners, and step up." They aren't owners… and they won't. This leader demonstrated amateur leader expectations, and no understanding of the use of conversation to clarify intention.

"If intention is anchored in flawed understandings, it will not be realized."

Recent research with over 2,000 employees across various industries, regions, and age groups by Paychex Works found that only roughly 63 percent of employees would leave their employment if overworked. (https://www.paychex.com/articles/human-resources/employee-retention-what-makes-employees-stay-leave) Boomers were the most likely to stay, and they are retiring in droves. Despite decades of experience that tells us otherwise, leaders persist in expecting that rational explanations (albeit, combined with cheerleading) will result in people becoming engaged, and willing to do more. This belief is wrong. Sadly, it took total failure, and much belated conversation, for our medical practice amateur leader to understand that his intentions were not aligned with those of staff. It was the leader who needed to change! Once leaders understood the underlying patterns in the practice, training was scheduled *during work time*, to enable staff learning. While costing a bit more in additional labor time, the implementation of the new system was rapid and well received by staff. To foster authentic engagement, it is necessary to align individual and organizational interests, so that people act and do what is best *because they want to.*

Panaceas, initiatives, experts, and solutions ... oh, my!

Years ago, one of my brothers announced that he had a new job in sales. He proudly clarified for our skeptical mother, "But I am not selling products. I am offering *solutions!*" Again, the man had intention! Our mom, a pragmatic and direct person, expressed pride in my brother's direction, and then turned aside, rolling her eyes for the rest of us to see. In her way of thinking, sales are sales, no matter what you call it. Today, most people with an address or phone number are being bombarded by countless offers for an amazing array of products and services, all masquerading as solutions to whatever problem emerges. Spam clutters email and sales agents pester via phone and text messages. Worse, in today's "techno-culture," simple things are no longer simple. The basic act of purchasing a cup of coffee presents a vast array of choices to be made. Everywhere, it seems, the "latest and greatest *that you must have"* are offered to assuage the anxiety you must be feeling because of the many unresolved problems you are faced with, day in and day out. And if you do not feel anxiety, those hawking products are quick to convince you that you should be. People today are "solution junkies," seeking quick fixes that are either unneeded, too expensive, or too complex for the "problems" being solved. Worse, many leaders have become addicted to data, speed, winning, power and control, approval, and a quest for perfection, making them easy prey for "teachers" and salespeople with the moral/ethical propensities of charlatans. One test to know if you are dealing with one is their insistence that you accept on faith, without question, what they are telling you to believe or do.

Throughout the '90s, leaders learned about CQI, TQM, process reengineering, quality circles, and "zero defects" as the latest quality-improvement methods. More recently, six sigma, branding, lean, ninety-day workouts, "out-of-the-box" customer service, and countless other solutions have been offered for application in the business. All of these initiatives have been billed as necessary leader strategies WITHOUT WHICH YOU

WILL LIKELY FAIL! They cost the buyers a great deal of money and foster obsessively reductive problem-solving methodologies fed by ignorance and simplistic notions. Yet evidence suggests that not much has been returned for the effort. Studies over the past few decades show that more than half of all such improvement efforts fail (Clemmer Group, 2001). The key factors named in these failures include complexity, priority collisions, piecemeal approaches (flow issues), improvement infrastructure with little accountability, failure to establish and maintain focus, inadequate training, and leadership who are not personally engaged (Antony & Gupta, 2019). In other words, nothing is wrong with the improvement methods and techniques being employed. But technique and tools masquerading as leadership are not leadership. We are plagued by amateurish leadership, falling prey to the "latest and greatest" magical solution. What is wrong is that intentions are not clear, not a priority, not shared, and not being led by professional leaders who can discern value. Leaders who do not know and communicate their purpose in clear, easy-to-understand terms cannot be trusted in their leadership. They will be dominated and driven by impulse and short-term self-interest, at the expense of everyone else.

"Technique and tools masquerading as leadership are not leadership."

What is *your* intention? Is it clear to those around you?

Spending time on purpose or vision statements often elicits cynicism in today's practical world of metrics and results. "We don't have time for that! There is real work to do!" Like most cynical reactions, this one is misplaced. "We have learned… that tangible vision is more than a nice-to-have idea; it is an essential part of the new leadership" (Bradford & Cohen, p. ix). Frankly, a vision that is unclear, ambiguous, and uncertain will lead to poor choices, weak energy, and even weaker execution. Every event is a moment of leadership opportunity. We are informed by our intentions, and how we act on them in the moment counts. Leading is more about keeping people connected to purpose, and less about solving problems or overcoming obstacles. Creating a vision, a clear statement of intention, clarifies a possible new reality, and establishes and defines the connections between people. Get past the hype about solutions and ask hard questions of yourself and of the people in your business. What matters most for your area of responsibility? For your organization and your customer? What specifically will you achieve that is not being accomplished today? What is your purpose as a leader in improving performance in your area of responsibility? If this possibility were to be real today, how would people behave? How would this change people, or the community? What matters most to you personally? The answers to these questions will not be handed to you. Find them in your experience, in your reflections, and in your conversations.

Having a clear vision changes leader behavior at a profound level. Bob, a key executive in a Fortune 100 client company, begins every meeting with the question "why are we here?" It's not rhetorical. He expects an answer and invites every member at the table to declare their purpose for the meeting. For those who do not understand the purpose, others are invited to explain. If there are different intentions, those differences are worked out. If the purposes of the meeting are insufficient to justify the time, the meeting is adjourned, or those who do not need to be there are dismissed. Everyone is clear on "why we are here." Some feel that this is harsh, but true purpose requires tenacity. Bob is being respectful and laser focused. Everyone on Bob's team truly understands the purposes of their work together, and what their specific part in that work is. Little stands in the way of this team accomplishing its intentions.

In your work, when you ask "Why are we here?" do you and your staff know the answer? Share your intentions, your ideas and beliefs. People need to hear your vision… from you, personally. And that alone is not enough. You need to listen to theirs as well! Amateurs tend to forget one basic rule: *the best way to accomplish your intentions is to help others accomplish theirs.*

True listening allows us to see the gifts others bring. But we must be available and open to the influence of others. This is an exchange best taken freely! Inviting people to co-author intention with you is the most powerful step you can take to bring about alignment. It provides "inside knowledge" about how to contribute and then take co-ownership. People will follow you not just because they understand what you intend to do, but because they feel you are partnering with them on their intentions, as well.

"The best way to accomplish your intentions is to help others accomplish theirs."

But be forewarned!

When creating a shared vision, it is likely that your original, "really great" vision will be distorted, "morphed" by the conversations. People may resist, and suggest amendments that surprise or even disturb you. Or they may not be able to see beyond the current state at all and be totally disinterested. It is difficult for people to imagine alternatives to what they have become accustomed to. Extraordinary leaders are willing to take this risk, and to do the hard work of conversation, exploration of new ideas, and learning required to foster shared vision. They move forward, and are never at the mercy of circumstances or the intentions of others. If the work or the people around you require you to move away from your own purpose, then something is amiss. Treat all of this as opportunity! Your task as leader is to align what people want with what needs to be done to fulfill the vision.

For intentional leaders, document creation is an important approach to fostering common vision and meaning, offering a bit of tangibility to the process. Writing it down, clarifying the words, and posting it for others to see and amend fosters understanding, creates energy, and sets the stage for commitment. Team charters, statements of expectation, compacts, business plans, roles and responsibilities, goals and intentions are all things that can be put in document form through robust, inspiring conversation. Extraordinary leaders understand that it is not the documents that are important, but engaging people in their co-creation that counts. Focus matters, and sometimes it is even advantageous to take people away from the worksite to have the conversations and create the understandings that are needed.

Intimidating with questions is not helpful, and not inspiring

Encountering obstacles in pursuing their vision, leaders often revert to inquiry for deeper insight. However, inquiry is a two-edged sword. It can be constructive as a learning process or intimidating, using very pointed questioning. Of course, amateur leaders would refer to pointed questions as "helping others understand," but, in reality, they are not. The questions take many forms: "Why is this an obstacle? Why are things this way? What is that about? Can you define the issue or obstacle in more detail? What is the explanation? Can you back up your hypothesis? What are the metrics that tell you this? Can you prove it? What does the data say? How much data did you collect, and do you need more? Why don't you explore a different approach?" (I know, Reader, that you may be thinking right now, "What is wrong with these questions?" Read on!) On their face, to the amateur leader these questions seem rational and appropriate. But context counts, and when the volume and pace rise, people shut down with such inquiry. Aggressive questions, disguised as innocent help, work at cross purposes to the vision, derailing the conversation quickly in what is really *an inquisition*, not an inquiry, and causing the person targeted to feel stupid and anxious. This is often an abusive means of avoiding conversation about what is most important. It is time to stop the punitive practices of fostering fear and submission to authority, and to embrace leadership as an inspirational practice.

Even if such questions are well-intentioned, we can usually learn what we need to know more effectively by watching, listening, and helping people inquire into their own reasoning. Effective leaders pose questions and observations with patience, gentle and caring guidance, and respectful permission for people to consider, to ask their own questions, and to come to their own conclusions. There are better, more respectful queries, if they are needed: "I see your situation… what does it mean to you? Help me understand your concerns. What are you experiencing? Tell me more. What are your biggest concerns? What would have to happen for you to be willing to go forward? And what am I missing that you see? What steps are you considering? And how can I help you?" And as they pursue such questions, extraordinary leaders search for, find, and exploit the positive in every situation, good or bad. Certainly, intentions should create energy, and perhaps a touch of anxiety, or they may not be big enough. But extraordinary leaders make sure that the energy is productive and the anxiety tempered.

"Extraordinary leaders realize that you should never expect people to accomplish goals and intentions that they cannot make their own."

So, the solutions are not "out there"— they are within

Achieving co-authored shared intention should be meaningful work. Psychologist Abraham Maslow (Maslow, 1943) taught that people work most diligently to serve their own "hierarchy of needs." They want opportunity to improve themselves for reasons of survival, security, ego, and meaning, and are willing to learn and change themselves for that to happen. This assumes that they have a say in how work is done, the pace of that work, and how that work promotes the larger achievement of the vision. It requires clear, meaningful conversation and respectful candor. Extraordinary leaders realize that you should never expect people to accomplish goals and intentions that they cannot make their own. The intentional leader has a clear choice… lead to serve their own needs and wants or lead to serve the needs and wants of those doing the daily work. Serving others will foster engagement in your shared purposes, while serving yourself will not. Serving others invites courage from those you are serving… they may follow, sometimes not even knowing why.

Extraordinary leaders see their jobs as much more than a title, an office, a phone, and a great paycheck. For the intentional leader, work is about mission and making choices, and investing what you have and who you are into service to others without expecting others to serve you in kind. You do what you do because it is worth doing, and if truth be told, work does not feel like work at all. Rather, it feels more like play. If we encounter a world of mess and problems to be solved, we can treat it as shabby, broken, and in need of repair… or as professionals, we can call it "in development," and do our part to build a better world. The first option is safe, in the comfort zone; the second option means creating something entirely new. One is self-imprisonment, the other, freedom and growth. Growth as an intentional leader means recognizing and confronting fears, deciding what you want and engaging fully in the work required to create depth of understanding and internal strength, not just in yourself, but in those around you. Change is often painful, and letting go is difficult, but required. If we allow our past experience to determine our future, we will never realize our possibilities… the past is over and done! Your best insights will come from stretching to achieve things that you've never accomplished before, and helping others stretch beyond their wildest expectations.

Two steps on the path to cultivating mindful intention

As you reflect on the messages in this chapter, consider how they apply to your leadership by answering and journaling the questions in Step 1, and by taking the challenges in Step 2. Record your learnings as you do this.

Step 1 (reflections and journaling):

> » What has been your experience in bringing about changes with staff that seemed logical and well planned? Did it go well, or was there resistance? Why?

» What matters most for your area of responsibility? For your organization, your staff, and your customer?

» What specifically will you achieve that is not being accomplished today? What is your purpose as a leader in improving performance in your area of responsibility?

» If this possibility were to be real today, how will people behave? How would this change people, or the community?

» How have you helped people see that their work is a mission? What matters most to you, personally? Do you and your staff know the answer to the question: "Why are we here?"

Step 2—Challenges: Vision is worthless if no one takes action to accomplish the vision. Take the following challenges in the spirit of "taking action" to make things extraordinarily more effective.

» Identify three areas of needed change in your area of work, and share them with staff, inviting input and conversation about the changes required.

» Enlist staff involvement in the planning and implementation of those changes, and learn from their observations and experience. Encourage them to own the changes, and the processes for bringing similar change about in the future.

» Explore ways to orchestrate resources and actions to make things happen faster.

» Set ambitious goals for each change, and then act! Observe the effect on staff.

» Maintain focus and priority until the changes are in place and normalized as daily work.

"If we allow our past experience to determine our future, we will never realize our possibilities."

» How long did it take, and why? What obstacles were encountered? What was done about them? What did you learn?

CHAPTER 3

Acting on Heart Intention (Care)

"The moment we agree to build a dream we don't believe in,
for whatever the reason, we become enslaved to the task."
—Nepo, 2005, p. 155

⚷ KEY POINTS SUMMARY

» Leaders must create and nurture vision with emotion and energy. Dream a little!

» To engage others in the vision, we must ask the right questions and invite co-authorship.

» The professional leader's job is to create an environment that enables personal accomplishment and joy in that accomplishment. This requires five promises.

» In the right environment, people gladly accept personal accountability.

I met Mary when she was a housekeeper in a small rural hospital, and I was engaged in service training for their managers. I had asked if anyone in the organization embodied the service mindset they were looking for, and everyone pointed toward Mary. So, I sought her out. One of her duties was to keep the emergency waiting room clean and tidy, and that is where I found her. Mary not only mopped floors, emptied baskets, dusted, and cleaned, she also served coffee to those waiting, took the time to talk with those who wished to talk, got them pillows and blankets, and found other ways to assist those who were there waiting. Understandably, the environment in a hospital ER is usually tense, but it seemed that Mary's presence came with a sense of peace in the room. I asked her what it was that caused so many people to name her as their service example. She was embarrassed by the question and a little perplexed, but told me with a smile, "I love these people. They are in pain, and if I can do small things to help them with that, I will. I am the hospital to these people when I am here, and I love doing what I do."

It gets even better. Her manager told me that she would do everything in her power to make sure that Mary had whatever she needed to do her job and to continue taking care of patients and their family members. Mary was known for her service in the community, and "greatly loved" for who she was. You don't often hear the word "love" used in a business setting. But it happens when extraordinary leaders are near.

Extraordinary leaders cultivate the possibilities that people like Mary bring. Exceptional results come from people like her who do what they do best, and what they love. Master leaders are first in offering respect and care for others, knowing that you cannot be respected without respecting others. This is emotional work. It is important that we not discount emotions in our work as leaders. Emotions are internal guidance systems, offering early notice that all is or is not well.

Mindful intention and heartfelt intention feed one another

"Positivity and negativity are a choice, not a result."

Leaders must be optimistic. The alternative is self-defeating. We can focus on thoughts of possible impending disaster, or on potential opportunities. This is a choice with clear consequences in our approach to life and work. Bold visions and intentions begin with possibility and a sense of passion. Without passion, you have a sterile goal with no emotional need to accomplish. Unfortunately, what often passes as vision sounds something like this (read in a slow monotone): "We will improve the performance of the department, and make sure that the customers' wants and needs are satisfied." What?! This is not a vision; it is more a form of bondage, a statement that likely will lead to status quo: no change and no energy. Where is the passion, the dream? Creating emotional energy means showing emotion in what you say and what you do. It is a choice to be energy-sharing or energy-depleting, open or closed, warm or cold. Positivity and negativity are a choice, not a result. Every leader has been given a personality through which they can energetically care for and about the people around them. Yet so many fail at this, opting instead for sterile focus on tasks and problems. In crafting our vision, it is not that we do not have desires but that our vision is too small, limited, and empty of emotional content. How about this vision, instead: *"We will radically improve the performance of our products and services, as measured by our customers, so that we capture an additional 30 percent of market share in two years, and never have to worry about our customers going to the competition or any of us losing our jobs"?* Whoa! That is an intention you can put your arms around! The differences are definable.

A heartfelt vision declares a *bold, ambitious* intention

Such vision is articulated in plain language, with unambiguous metrics and timelines, and creates an emotional connection. Emotional energy is seldom found in complexity. It is found in simplicity. A simple, bold vision describes a profoundly different reality than what exists today, in emotional terms. Few will be inspired or will become emotionally engaged in logical or ambiguous plans and exercises, or financially based metrics that slash costs and people, create anxiety, or speak only to the organization's internal purposes. Amateur leaders often treat such rational and boring intentions as if they have somehow come from God, rather than from their own ambition. Being this self-obsessed is limiting, preventing learning that comes from living life. Our future is less tied to the need for sterile information and more dependent on the need for us to acknowledge and engage one another on an emotional level. Greater *shared purpose* is required for heartfelt intention to be exciting. Richard Leider (Leider, p. 21) affirms that "the failure of many organizations to enlist people in some kind of unselfish, non-quantitative purpose is at the root of many productivity problems today." The message for leaders is to imagine specifically what you want, together with the people around you . . . fill that space with possibility and challenges that matter, or it will be filled by what you do not want. Share with others what you want emotionally, and encourage others to do likewise.

So, how does a leader create shared, heartfelt intention?

This is a little like asking "How do I dream?" and the questions are related. The beginning of a vision is a dream. For some, it is more natural; for others, it defies logic. But there are five steps that can help in the vision-creating process, whether done individually or in a group setting. Try this:

1. *Think big!* What would a perfect world look like? What would perfect customers look like? How would they act? What would happen if your processes and products were perfect? And if everything worked as it should, what would be the perfect payoff?

2. *Write the ideas down!* Put your big ideas in writing on a simple piece of paper, or flip-chart it, using Post-its so that you can easily group and change things.

3. *Grow and harden your big ideas with specific detail and depth.* What are the tangibles? Can you see it, hear it, taste it, smell it, or feel it? How will you feel in this environment?

4. *Let your big ideas simmer in reality...* what is within possibility, and what is outside of possibility? Let the ideas steep for a while. As you do, winnow the list down to two or three bold "stretch" statements without ambiguity. And make sure they are emotional.

5. **And most important**, *walk the ideas around for conversation!* Extraordinary leaders know that great things happen when people come together in conversation. Everything that you bring to the conversation is based on your collective thoughts, thoughts that you choose. If you are changing or expanding your vision, you must expand your thoughts! Expose your vision to others in person, not by email, not by memo, not by phone. Authentic engagement with others happens in the relationship, in the being together, not in the doing. "Doing" is never sufficient if we neglect being, paying attention to one another personally in the formation of the vision, being present as it evolves. How would staff interact and get the vision accomplished? What would they do to make it better? How would they expand it or make it more tangible? How would they tame it? Ask them, and build their ideas into it so that they can see their contributions as a collective vision. Give them the opportunity to experience the vision as their own.

> *"Great things happen when people come together in conversation."*

Inexperienced leaders often hesitate to allow others in, fearing judgment of their dreams. They are convinced that certain goals must be met, certain processes employed, and that everything must stay in control. But it is possible that keeping things obsessively in order and under control robs us of opportunities even greater. All people bring gifts and capabilities, and most are honored when asked for their insight. With emotions and relationships, what matters most is openness, care, and truth. Jeff, an information technology supervisor, held a secret desire (his personal vision) to become the executive in charge of that area. When asked, he admitted that he had not told anyone in leadership about his aspirations. But within eight years of mustering up the courage to declare his intentions in a caring, helpful way and enlisting others in his personal intentions, he became the CIO of that organization. Be careful what you dream about—it might happen! When you involve others, you are gifting them with energy and intention, and can accomplish beyond anything you thought possible.

Sharing the vision and creating shared expectations

Creating a clear intention is not enough. The effective leader must invite *others* to focus action on that intention (remember the kiosk in Chapter 2?), and often in a climate that is not always receptive to easy agreement. We cannot make others be more engaged than they are any more than we can will our own spouses, children, or significant others to be more attentive to our needs. Doing so only creates pain and disorder by insisting on how things ought to be, robbing people of their own emotional flow. In fact, research suggests that engagement in corporate America is declining, despite decades of surveys and initiatives focused on improving engagement. According to the Hay Group, median employee turnover rates were roughly 12 percent in 2012. In its 2017 global survey (http://www.aon. com/unitedkingdom/attachments/trp/2017-Trends-in-Global-Employee-Engagement.pdf), AON Hewitt reported: "Just 24 percent of all employees fall into the Highly Engaged category and another 39 percent can be categorized as Moderately Engaged." A 2013 Gallup survey (https://www. gallup.com/corporate/212381/who-we-are.aspx) revealed that, globally, an incredible 87 percent of workers are "not engaged in their work with 24 percent actively disengaged, while only 13 percent were engaged!" They figure that the consequence of this in the US is roughly $550 billion in lost productivity!

It appears that current management trends are working against inspiration. Leaders who motivate by "creating burning platforms" (Who wants to come to work to have their "platform" set on fire?!) and other forms of manipulation will not succeed, and will likely do damage. People reduced to anxiety and fear have a reduced capacity for caring, love, integrity, and self-worth. They begin to withdraw, hide mistakes, and misrepresent facts, keeping things risk free because trying something new may leave them open to criticism. All of this makes employees hesitant to discuss problems with others, for fear they will leave themselves open to ridicule (Sonnenberg, 2012).

Engagement requires that you be attentive to others, focusing on aligning people who want to succeed. Creating emotional alignment as a competency is not something that can be learned by following a standardized checklist of actions and behaviors. An emotional competency that appeals to people's hearts requires interpersonal savvy, compassion, intuition, a degree of spontaneity, and a true interest in the welfare of the people you are inspiring—traits that require true caring and deliberate practice over time.

So, how do you go about inspiring people to follow your vision with full understanding of what is expected of them along the way? Leaders have choices: To organize leadership intention around meeting needs and deficiencies (weaknesses) or to organize around possibility (strength). You can choose to create fear and anxiety, or challenge and excitement. And you can choose to focus first on limits and constraints, or on opportunity and abundance. The most effective leaders inspire with possibility, validate

"Your intentions create reality, so be careful about what you project."

strengths, and identify the abundance available to accomplish intention. Your intentions create reality, so be careful about what you project. What is heard by others is often different than what is meant. When we praise, it can sometimes feel like patronization, rather than validation. When we give advice, it can often feel like criticism. And when we criticize, it can be perceived as punishment. This is not to say that leaders should choose to be naïve about deficiencies or to "walk on eggs" with their staff. But they must assess limits and risk, and be able to address concerns with candor, as opportunities for growth, creativity, and learning.

Motivating Others:

If there is a secret to motivating others, it is simple: *most people are already motivated*, and want to contribute good work. The story about Mary at the beginning of this chapter is a case in point. Mary was self-motivated. But you, as leader, must make the connection between their dreams and yours. Speak about your intentions in their language, and link to their loves, hopes, and dreams. Only then will others freely engage in what you must achieve. This is emotional work linked to the rational thinking process, and people become emotionally attached to what they create together. This, and small daily acts of appreciation and acknowledgment, do more for cultivating pride and engagement in work than any big award or bonus. It is the daily act that cultivates relationships. It also takes imagination, which does not reside in your rational self but in your emotional self, and is unleashed in conversation with people you care about. It is in the conversation that you create new dreams, heal the wounds of past disappointment, find out who you really are, and declare what you want. Rather than trying to change others to your point of view (an amateur approach), be willing to change yourself and how you engage with others (the master's approach). When you allow yourself to see from perspectives other than your own, you are defining yourself as an extraordinary leader, willing to learn and grow, willing to be influenced, and open to discovery of new possibility through layers of conditioning and social expectations.

Reality dose—it's foolish to think you can change things without causing disruption, even chaos. And you won't inspire everyone! Sharing your vision and inviting others to contribute to it require courage. But as Isaacs (Isaacs, p. 162) insists, "Only as you learn to take seriously the possibility that what you think might in fact be valid for others do you find the backbone and confidence to share it." But once you share the vision with others, not everyone will be inspired to support it. Some are rebels, who will disagree with the vision overtly, or even covertly, refusing to align their behaviors. There are also cynics and naysayers, who tend to carry a great deal of anger and disappointment, with little trust in their leaders. Any change will create challenges, and challenges create energy, both positive and negative. Change is never linear. Perhaps some resist because the leader is not listening… do you really listen without rebuttal or defense? Do you find yourself interrupting others, or hurrying them along? Is it all mind and no heart? Listening is a deep dance, felt in the heart and gut as a connection, never as a judgment.

"If there is a secret to motivating others, it is simple: most people are already motivated, and want to contribute good work."

Cultivating a workforce with heartfelt intention

The conditions for an engaged workforce have been known for decades and are fairly simple. At the most fundamental level, operant conditioning confirms that, like all living creatures, people seek pleasure and avoid pain, moving toward those things they want, like, and need, and repeating behaviors that bring pleasure. People move away from those things that make them uncomfortable, create frustration, and that they dislike. Further, human beings take pleasure in being part of something great, and will even endure discomfort to get it! People generally want five promises from their leaders before they will engage fully from the heart: 1) I will work to help you achieve your dreams and share my dreams with you; 2) I will help you grow and learn, and learn along with you; 3) I will celebrate your successes and have your back when things get difficult; 4) We can always talk… I will listen; 5) I will always tell you my truth, no spin, and will always respect your truth. These promises set a relationship context that allows the risk of vulnerability that comes with truth-telling and commitment to a vision. Rapid cooperative engagement cannot occur except in a climate of trust and mutual respect. Period! The greatest damage of a broken promise is not the failure itself but the damage to trust that has been broken. When making promises, be straightforward, use no "waffle words," and treat everything and everyone with respect.

None of this is difficult to understand, yet many amateur leaders miss the point. They think that they must exercise authority, demand, cajole, preach, and use discipline to get people to do unpleasant tasks, organize their lives around business events, accept priorities and standardized processes not of their making, sacrifice time for self and family—and do it all with good cheer and high levels of energy. All of this leads to transactional relationships and reliance on rules and policy that have little spirit and impede our sense of being alive. If you focus on making demands on others, you will eventually find yourself meeting the demands of others as a constant part of the transaction. If your focus is on being of service to others, you will find others working to be of service to you.

Being inspired and inspiring is not soft!

Inspiring people to achieve a vision through emotional connection is not a soft, naïve approach to leadership. Part of adult maturation is being more able to express feelings in an authentic way. And those who do not accept and respect your feelings are not friends. Inspiration requires resolve, understanding that eventually it may be necessary to remove some from your organization because they will not align (discussed more in depth in Chapter 8).

Building an emotionally rewarding, productive environment, where people are engaged in the work while satisfying themselves in the process, is not easy, nor is it simple. Sometimes, the right course of action may be to undo that which no longer works. While we crave the ideal, more importantly, we must insist on the real. William Bridges, in his work on transformation and change (Bridges, p. 37), teaches that "there is, in fact, no right way, for every way has its price and its rewards." The goal is to build a self-directed, self-correcting, and self-improving community of extraordinary professionals who love their work and who get the work done with a minimum amount of supervision and with a great deal of freedom in the use of professional judgment regarding the resources at their disposal. This requires leader awareness and emotional skill to navigate respectful relationships, and to provide information, authority, resources, and the will to insist on measurably high performance in a positive setting over time. Real meaning and intention can only come in relation to others. Leadership mastery, like friendship, means connecting your life to the lives of others through sharing, helping, trusting, and engaging with them in the endeavors that enrich their lives. Neither your destiny nor your legacy is determined by the routine work you do every day. Rather, who you are and what you leave behind come from your decisions and your heart.

"Those who do not accept and respect your feelings are not friends."

Two steps on the path to cultivating heartfelt intention

Leading from the heart is a practice that requires time, relational experience, a bit of humility, and reflection. Take to heart this quote from Maya Angelou (as quoted in Moore, p. 95): "I've learned that people will forget what you said, people will forget what you did, but people will never forget how you made them feel." As you reflect on the messages in this chapter, consider how this applies to your leadership by answering the questions in Step 1, and by taking the action challenges in Step 2. Meet with people, listen to what matters most to them, and journal your learnings.

Step 1 (reflections and journaling):

» Why are the people in my charge choosing the work of their professions? Do I know their reasons, or care? What if I did?

» Name three things my staff do unconsciously well. What are the success stories? Has their work been organized around that? And have they been acknowledged for that contribution?

» Do people feel that they have the authority, knowledge, and resources to accomplish extraordinary things? If not, why?

» Am I using fear or possibility in my motivational work with staff? How?

» How are current reward systems helping? How do they hurt?

» Who are the three staff most in need of support in making a "breakthrough" in their work? What do those staff need from me, right now?

» How can I create an environment of learning, growth, and personal accountability for extraordinary results?

Step 2—Taking Action: The action challenge assignment for this chapter is simple: spend time and talk with three people working in your area of responsibility about your dreams and goals. In fact, don't just talk. Listen to them, too. Ask them about their dreams and goals, write down what they tell you, and then find something in that to act on. Today!

» What makes them proud in their work, and gives them energy?

» Do they know your vision, and their role in accomplishing that vision?

» Do they know that you care about them? How do they know?

» What depletes their energy?

» What two things can you do to help them achieve extraordinary results for the organization, and for them individually in their own lives? Make promises to them that you will help them succeed, then keep the promises.

» Take the five steps in crafting a shared vision with your staff:

> *Create a big idea!* What would a perfect world look like? What would perfect customers look like? How would they act? How would staff interact, and get their work done? And if everything worked out, what would be the perfect payoff?

> *Write it down!* Put your big idea in writing.

> *Feed the big idea with specific detail and depth.* What are the tangibles? Can you see it, hear it, taste it, smell it, or feel it?

> *Let the big idea simmer for a bit in reality*—what is within possibility and what is outside it? Create two or three bold "stretch" statements without ambiguity. Make sure they are emotional.

> *Walk the idea around with others for conversation and perspectives.* Let others inform the big idea, challenge the assumptions, and add their perspectives. Foster co-authorship!

CHAPTER 4

Acting on Spirit Intention (Purpose)

"What kind of world have we created where the simple speaking of the truth, as we see it, is seen as courageous?"
—Anne Wilson Schaef

🔑 KEY POINTS SUMMARY

» The professional leader works to create the expectation of integrity, honesty, and candor. In-spirit intention begins with truth.

» Honest work that contributes meaning and value to others can be a source of great meaning and purpose, but the inspired leader must nurture that result.

» Leading from spirit means ensuring that those doing the work accomplish their intentions and feel genuine gratitude for doing so.

» Being in spirit is neither rational nor emotional... it emanates from intuition and imagination. Recognize that meaning is experienced as a long-term goal.

The world of work is changing. Many people are no longer satisfied with working for a paycheck and benefits. They long for work that offers purpose, a chance to make things better. Some seem to think that inspiration is something that happens before the work is started. Such thinking will require a lot of waiting, and not much worth doing will get done! Waiting to make changes "because we or circumstances are not ready" is our excuse. Such waiting is not "owning the room." Most great accomplishments begin before people are ready. As every creative artist knows from experience, inspiration happens *in the work*, and in the interchange between people. Sometimes it must germinate over time, measured in months and years to be realized.

Neil was a quiet, pleasant guy, a fifteen-year HR employee who kept to himself. His job included predicting future staffing needs, recruiting talent, orchestrating the hiring and orientation processes to get people off to a good start, and working closely with managers during that activity. But Neil was a mediocre performer at best, and in some areas, he was failing to meet the needs of the operational managers, causing repeated unfilled job vacancies, dissatisfied managers, and criticism of the entire human resources function. Despite many conversations about what was required and possible improvements to resolve the complaints, Neil was not getting the message, so I scheduled lunch with him. Surprisingly, Neil began our conversation with an unexpected declaration. "I believe it's time for you to give me a raise." I was stunned! What had gone so wrong? How could Neil have possibly considered this lunch an opportunity to ask for a raise? What didn't he understand about his performance after the many coaching sessions and suggestions? Not once did it occur to me that perhaps *I* did not understand the situation.

I pointed out again that there were performance issues and repeated failures on his part to do what was required for success, and therefore, there was no raise on the horizon. Rather, his job was in jeopardy. With what appeared to be a sigh of relief, Neil disclosed that he disliked doing his job, that he was "bored stiff," and that he had no idea why he had entered human resources in first place. I asked him what he loved doing, and what he said surprised me again. "Carpentry! I love working with my hands." Over five years in that department, I never had a clue about how uncomfortable Neil was. And more surprising, until that moment, neither did Neil!

One of the greatest barriers to success as a leader is a failure to be true to your spirit and honest about the situation. When the business is failing, the customer unhappy, and staff doesn't want to be there, amateur leaders often hold onto the idea that they are actually competent leaders, maybe even great ones, regardless of the circumstances they have before them and of their own contribution to the problems. The "inner critic" described by Julia Cameron in *Finding Water* (2006) emerges, keeping the leader focused on problem-solving while blaming circumstances and others instead of exploring new pathways. This critic shuns creativity and its imperfections in favor of the familiar, despite the results. An absence of self-reflection dooms such leaders to continued mediocrity, frustration, and eventually, boredom. Big changes require that we give up what we know in favor of possibility that comes with much unknown. But this is how big things happen! Boredom, in essence, is an insult to oneself. Being "bored stiff" is a rehearsal for death. You never want to go there!

"Big changes require that we give up what we know in favor of possibility that comes with much unknown."

The truth is the truth

Neil's story is about the truth being the truth—authenticity. For years, he had been favoring certainty over uncertainty while his spirit, or sense of purpose, knew better. From our conversation, it became apparent it was time to shift to what he desired authentically. Today's world is insane at times, forcing reaction to incessant, unrealistic demands on time and energy. Focus is on task rather than outcome, threatening to imprison the leader in never-ending process and protocol. We are conditioned to make decisions based on what we think we are supposed to do, rather than on what we want, or even need, to do. Intuitive truth is distrusted in favor of data-based truth. Somehow, objectivity and rationality are deemed more important than "the truth," which always contains a point of view. People are constantly told what to think and do as somebody's conception of "common sense," none of which is living from the heart. Additionally, our world is increasingly divided, with focus more on our differences rather than on what is in common. In our science-dominated world, we have somehow come to believe that the study of the behavior of rats is somehow superior to our own intuition in understanding the human being, and this should give us all pause. We seem to think that we can address the significant human problems in our work with engineering solutions. But the human spirit is about wonder, gratitude, unconditional respect, serenity, authenticity, and connection, just to name a few characteristics. Inspired leaders cut across divisions, bringing people together to accomplish great things. Extraordinary leaders value discovery as much as calculation, harmony as much as productivity, and intuition as much as reason. The rational among us struggle with accepting or valuing intuition because it is difficult to measure or parse, and therefore deemed less trustworthy. But extraordinary professionalism and authenticity require the courage to keep the human enterprise in priority.

Like many, Neil mapped out his career as a young man. Young people make many decisions about life direction and the skills, knowledge, and relationships needed for success. They also take buckets of advice from well-meaning parents, relatives, and friends, all claiming to have their best interests in their hearts but who in fact have their own ideas about how the world should work. All of this is fairly natural and helpful during the maturation process for children, but when adults continue to rely on external forces (family, schooling, religion, government) to provide meaning, the very foundation of their own spirit is denied. According to Vishen Lakhiani, it is time to challenge the "brules" (Lakhiani, 2016, p. 21) that he defines as "the bulls**t rules we adopt to simplify our understanding of the world." It is in the human spirit that personal power resides, not in the "brules." Growth occurs in your taking responsibility for becoming what you must become, irrespective of the advice and good intentions of others, no matter who they are. Our leadership should never be determined by what others tell us we should do. The most powerful agent for personal transformation is letting go of the approval of others and acknowledging who you are. Neil was still living his career based on the decisions his younger self, an immature twenty-year-old, made and he hated it. He had been living a lie, and it was now time for the thirty-five-year-old to take charge and listen to his inner voice. He had the courage to be authentic with me, and it was now my job to respectfully help him, without judgment.

"Our leadership should never be determined by what others tell us we should do."

What is the inspiring (in spirit) professional leader?

Human beings are profoundly different than machines, and must be approached with deeper, more human ways of response. To work in an environment that is highly scripted and externally focused is to lose touch with your own spirit, your own internal intentions. The perfectionistic mantra is "standardize" the process, which admittedly offers short-term efficiency and control, but at what expense? We human creatures are not robots. Are creative thoughts and approaches really that dangerous? People who submit to such control for long become numb to life following thoughtless processes, or go crazy.

Mindful intention, paired with heartfelt action, opens the channels, allowing connection to the human spirit for larger purpose. Extraordinary leaders are "in spirit" and know who they are as human beings with the self-discipline to lead with their "higher" selves. Despite anger, they lead with compassion. Despite anxiety, they lead with confidence. And despite the jealousies of competition, they lead with unity of spirit. Such professionalism is the foundation for credibility, earned through authenticity. Humans as children begin in a state that is authentic: genuine, sincere, legitimate, and true to self. We are then immersed in a world of denial, labeling, politics, and spin, with some people even capable of lying to gain attention. All is rationalized in the name of practicality: "going along to get along." People stray from their core values or principles and become less than authentic for two reasons: immediate gratification and conformity. As leaders, we must be the ones who aim for excellence and inspire others to do so as well. Extraordinary leaders never let others criticize them for following their own vision, intuition, and desires. They set their own course and encourage others to set their own as well. They are acutely aware of the effects that their energy and attention have on others, both mentally and emotionally, an awareness that can only come from self-reflection. Authentic leaders help people know that they are part of something bigger than themselves, while doing or being themselves in their achievements and accomplishments. They have the wisdom to know when to seize new opportunities, and the gentle courage to say "no" to bright, shiny distractions. Such authenticity is unscripted, meaning that you engage another without pre-thought, without knowing what you will say, and allowing the heart as much play as the head.

So, what must occur to nurture credibility and the capacity for open, honest, and straightforward relationships? Kouzes and Posner conducted research in the mid-eighties on credibility among leaders (Kouzes & Posner, p. 14), and found that certain characteristics are common for those who were considered most credible: honesty, forward-looking, inspiring, competent, and fair-minded. It would be wise to begin here. Authenticity happens in relationships, in being together, not in the completion of tasks. This means paying attention to one another, being present.

People seek purpose beyond self and, finding it, thrive. Without it, we focus only on our tasks at hand, on immediate desires and wants, and these are fleeting at best, leaving us empty. Until we find true meaning and dignity in our work and lives, we will be at the mercy of momentary wants and needs, mostly pseudo-purpose. Our friend Neil from earlier in the chapter is not alone in how he has navigated his life and career. Many in their forties, fifties, and older are living their lives like him, based on decisions made by twenty-something adults who have not yet experienced the many nuances of life. Likewise, many of most leaders' basic practices are the result of learning and experiences that were formed years, perhaps decades, ago. Intentional spirit leadership requires a deeply profound honesty about who you are *today*, what you now stand for, what your weaknesses are, what your strengths are, and what you intend. Such authenticity is both liberating and painful. It requires a great deal of personal reflection and feedback from others because it challenges you to refuse to lie and to confront yourself in uncommon ways. Times of pain and discomfort can be powerful for achieving growth and change. Most of what leaders do is not difficult. What is difficult is getting into a state of mind to do what is needed to cultivate purpose and meaning. It takes courage to break the chains of the past and chart a new course.

"It takes courage to break the chains of the past and chart a new course."

After learning about his woodworking dreams, I offered to help Neil find a new role in which he could do work he truly loved. I promised him that, because of his long service to the organization, he would be treated respectfully. Neil left that lunch without his raise, but with a smile on his face. Six months later, after a transfer, he was working in our organization as a carpenter, and loving every bit of it.

So, how do in-spirit leaders behave?

Leading from spirit is not about being informed, or informing others. Neither is it about emotional empathy or caring, though these traits help. Leading from spirit is about purpose and meaning, and inspiring others to achieve same. There are aspects of this that cannot be easily written into a business plan or to-do list. To find our spirit, we first must ease up on anxious rationalism, give play to intuition and imagination, and allow human experience into the work flow. The more rational among us will confess to being uncomfortable with that, and even insist on more tangibility, more "evidence-based" work leading to measurable outcomes. We love to be comfortable… but it is the courage to face discomfort that enables growth that results in life experience. In our overly metric-driven business pursuits, we have somehow allowed the human energy that pursues meaning to go unheeded. Improving the company bottom line is not a terribly motivating purpose for most. The human spirit does not come alive in the one-dimensional practicalities of daily life, but rather in the sacred moments in which we realize our own purposes. People generally aren't with you merely because they want to survive and help the company. They want challenge, acknowledgment, purpose, appreciation, and even love. They want to be known, and to do things that matter.

An amateur leader might conclude from this that it would be wise to establish a goal to become more "in spirit." Don't do it! Professional leaders know that leading from spirit is neither a goal, nor a set of specific behaviors. Rather it is an openness to promptings from our centered selves, our "gut feelings." In-spirit leaders understand that there are certain definable (but maybe not measurable) skills involved. These include reflection, particularly self-reflection, mindfulness, intuition, detachment from outcomes, and creative imagination. They view leaders as "witnesses" and observers, rather than as drivers and task managers. They realize that many things about leading from spirit can only be affirmed in experience, and not proven—things like kindness, connection, love, and innumerable other traits that we relegate to the world of feelings. Above all, in-spirit leaders lead with gratitude, never control.

People require order to feel balanced

A world of rapid change and uncertainty throws people off balance, and constant chaos can be demoralizing. Effective leaders understand this, and provide inspiration, order, priority, clear intention, and the confidence to live with tension. Doing this well over time requires leaders who are centered, and who have a profound understanding of the human experience that goes beyond the daily task work and rational problem-solving. People do not really want complete freedom in such an environment. We are "wired" to be interdependent, communal, and sharing creatures, and we crave leaders who can bring order and structure to the shifting environment.

But people do not want to be boxed in, either. Do the structures and rules of our work environment enable us or impede us? Being over-controlled is an energy drain, creating diminished satisfaction, often resentment, and frustration. What people need is the autonomy to be the writers of their own stories, within a stable, nurturing organization. The guidelines and rules of life are meant to adapt to changing circumstances. To be effective, extraordinary leaders know that they must be willing to challenge them, and never accept rules designed to encourage mindless effort (Lakhiani, 2016). In addition, people want their leaders to inspire possibility (Leider, 2004). Authentic, spirit-driven leaders trust that resources are plentiful, even inexhaustible. There are no limits in the exercise of creativity, cooperation, and the pursuit of purpose and service to others. Those who choose to lead from pessimism rather than optimism, worrying over limited resources, possible changes in plans, negative feedback, and so on, doom themselves to defeat. They expect and prepare for the worst and hope for the best… this is so backward! The professional leader begins with optimism, preparing for the best, calculating risk, and moving forward with intention, knowing that inspired people bring a power and energy that cannot be contained once unleashed. Optimism matters. Are we doing things

"What people need is the autonomy to be the writers of their own stories, within a stable, nurturing organization."

to become happy? Or are we bringing our happiness and joy to the work? People who are in balance simply do not worry much.

Building an environment of in-spirit accomplishment

Inspired wisdom teaches us that the sacred is right here, right now, and if we cannot see it right before us, our travels around the world will not change anything. Creating an authentic workplace, with people doing the right work at the right time in the right way *because they want to,* is an in-spirit accomplishment. In an authentic environment, it is not enough to be a good person. Beyond good, you must face yourself as you really are:—strengths, weaknesses, desires, and needs—and be reality-based in your approaches to accomplishment. In addition, master leaders know that they must live and work only with those who inspire dreams and who can bring calm in chaos. They value creativity, and know that creative people require time and an environment in which they can simmer and grow. They never settle for living in fear of failure, or fear of what others might think or do. When extraordinary leaders "own the room" with passionate intentions, "OK" results are never sufficient. The courage to be great is not innate. It is a decision waiting to be made, and when you make it, you'll probably be alone. For the extraordinary leader, it is more about significance (making a difference) than it is about success (achieving goals). They know that people who lead in spirit will be challenged, and maybe even "pummeled" by those who are more rational or emotional in approach. They also know that they must take care of their own balance, and perhaps take periodic excursions outside of the daily routine to refresh, re-energize, and renew. You cannot achieve balance through attempts to control your external world. Rather, you must create an inner world that supports your efforts. Inspired leaders seek out friends with whom they can share such "inner-world" excursions.

You cannot accomplish much through rational work alone. Real accomplishment requires imagination, creativity, and courage, along with a tenacity to get things done. Further, leader authenticity is not measured by *what* is accomplished but by *how* it is accomplished. At the highest levels of mastery, leaders see that what they are engaged in has little to do with specific outcomes or rewards, and everything to do with the quality of relationships and life itself. In-spirit leaders are open to everything and attached to nothing. When life changes the circumstances, we can beg, and rail at reality... or we can move forward and take responsibility for our own choices. It is the leader's job to create that environment, to nurture and reinforce it in whatever way possible. That is how you own the room! If you do not, the rational role of leadership will likely bring you to your knees. This is no place for amateurs!

"The courage to be great is not innate. It is a decision waiting to be made, and when you make it, you'll probably be alone."

Two steps on the path to cultivating in-spirit intention

Leading from spirit is a practice that requires respect for the truth, a trust in your intuition, and a measure of creative imagination. As you reflect on the messages in this chapter, consider how they apply to your leadership by answering the questions in Step 1, and by taking the action challenges in Step 2. Take time to reflect, listen internally to what matters most to you, and journal what you are learning as you do this.

Step 1:

» What has been your path to where you are today? Did you follow your own passions or those of well-meaning people in your life? Do you feel passion today?

» What three things in your life are feeding your spirit? How do you know?

» What are you doing to make space for yourself?

> » As a leader, are you pursuing "the good life," or a life of goodness? There is a big difference! Would others describe you as inspiring? Would they consider you authentic? Why or why not?

Step 2:

> » *Open an internal dialogue with yourself.* Write down your core purpose and values, fears, issues, and concerns. Then put that away for a short time. Then retrieve it, and offer advice from your higher self, as if you were advising a friend.

> » *Amplify your intuition.* Get rest, eat the healthiest foods you can find, pay attention to your feelings and emotions, and open your heart to everything that comes your way in life and work. Trust what you experience.

> » *Ask those around you who inspires them.* Ask why and take note.

> » *Do an act of kindness every day.* Give a gift, big or small. Express gratitude to someone every day.

> » *Take a walk with no purpose or destination.* Just experience the walk.

CHAPTER 5

Leadership is Not for Amateurs!

"If your actions inspire others to dream more, learn more, do more and become more, you are a leader."
—John Quincy Adams

🗝 KEY POINTS SUMMARY

» Being a leader is about the choices we make.

» Characteristics of high-performing extraordinary leaders.

» Leadership poisons: today's world tends to feed anxiety and stress, taking our attention away from things that matter most and causing focus on control rather than purpose.

» Extraordinary leaders help others in personal transformation.

» Intentional leadership means cultivating credibility and engagement.

In the past few chapters, the focus has been on each of three essential leadership practices: leading from the mind (intention), from the heart (care), and from spirit (purpose). But these are not separate and distinct activities that can be easily parsed and segmented as we work with people every day. Rather, they work together as a flow in response to an environment that is constantly changing and presenting new challenges. We love it when things go well. But we hate it when things go wrong, and this is where extraordinary leaders excel. Things will always go wrong... that's life! The challenge is to turn "wrong" into opportunity. To do so, our intentions must be in balance... mind, heart, and spirit. When out of balance, we are out of flow, favoring mind over heart or heart over spirit. Extraordinary leaders deal with change much differently than amateurs. They know that to grow and transform, they must accept the basic reality of change, and abandon the expectation of security. Transformation means moving into the unknown. In this chapter, we will put it all together to see "the whole."

Being a high performance, authentic leader is a choice

Accepting any leadership responsibility is a choice. A prerequisite for that choice is the decision to inspire others to follow, by exercising mind, heart, and spirit in one motion. You can be a leader or a follower... both legitimate and useful roles. If you accept leadership responsibility, there are more choices. This is not for sissies! You are leading people who have their own goals, needs, personalities, opinions, feelings about how things should be, and abilities to make free choices. Will you do what it takes to master the practices of mind, heart, and spirit intentional leadership? Or will you base your leadership only on what you have learned along the way through experience and serendipity, trusting that that is sufficient to do what is required to lead? The former is the beginning of mastery, the latter is amateur. Unfortunately, many choose the latter, either out of laziness or naiveté. For some, it is just plain ego that prevents an in-depth study of what a true master leader is. They are more interested in *how* they are doing (ego) than *what* they are doing (results/contribution). If any of this describes you, your beliefs about leadership are at risk, because you have not taken the time to define them. You must reflect and know what you believe from your head, heart, and spirit.

We know this: intentional leaders set high expectations for themselves and for those around them. They cultivate a culture of high performance, nourish an abundance mindset, establish a framework of professionalism and respect, and communicate in all directions with transparency and energy... just a few of the responsibilities! Leaders who come into leadership without grounding in how these things are done are woefully unprepared for what they are about to experience. Mastery of this requires time, attention, courage, and tenacity, and without these traits, none of the other leadership characteristics or skills are sustainable.

"Things will always go wrong... that's life! The challenge is to turn 'wrong' into opportunity."

This is not for amateurs!

Another story: the staff were angry, and wanted to talk. (Actually, they really wanted to rant, shout, and scream!) I was invited by the manager of these ninety transcriptionists to help them understand why their jobs were in jeopardy due to technology changes (a company decision to transition to voice technology for transcription services). I soon learned that they were angry about many different things. Some had invested years of training and experience in their profession, and now felt obsolete. Others were angry that management had withheld information about this change until merely weeks prior to it, meaning they had little time to react. Still others were upset that the organization had not given any thought to what could be done to retrain these staff for other roles in the organization. Recent open positions they could have filled were no longer available. Their anger was legitimate, and it was clear that the changes had been poorly orchestrated—a leadership failure. The room was literally filled with angry thoughts, and angry thoughts do not lead to productive ends.

All results begin with our thoughts. If thoughts are positive, they will breed results that are positive. If they are negative, they will breed negative results. It can't work any other way. There are many telltale signs when dealing with amateur leaders, signs most professionals will recognize immediately. Amateurs, particularly those who come from technical professions and those with "working supervisor" titles, tend to see leadership as secondary to their "real job" or as a part-time function. They often do leadership work because their personality is more dominant, or because no one else will step forward. The work gets done when "I get around to it" or only when inspired to focus on it, frustrating those waiting for results. It seems that we have given "managerial leaders" an impossible task: stabilize the organization, and keep it under control, while at the same time profoundly change things to generate significant improvement in business results. Some leaders, as in our transcriptionist scenario, submit to the obsessions of perfectionism and fast results, insisting that everything be done a certain way, at a certain time, to a certain standard, in the best interests of the organization—no exceptions, without regard for the people impacted. Amateur leaders conserve power to themselves rather than share it. And when communicating tough messages, they tend to try to put a positive spin on things to avoid difficulty or pain.

As a consultant who provides a great deal of coaching feedback to executives and managers at all levels, I know that amateur leaders love it when they're praised and hate criticism, responding with defensiveness and sometimes even retaliation. Amateurs avoid risk as much as possible, deferring tough decisions to others or procrastinating until circumstances decide for them. Amateurs often see the world as a very political place, and attempt to navigate the politics as a win/lose game that must be played for success. To the amateur, respect and trust must be earned before they are given, and when things go wrong, someone must be found to blame. In the amateur world, leaders measure process and how hard people are working, rather than outcomes and results. Amateur leaders are often proud of being promoted into leadership from the ranks, without formal leadership training, and take failure very personally. To the amateur leader, resources are limited and pessimism is more realistic than optimism. Where can such thinking lead but to negative results?

Many of these thoughts were at work in the transcription case, producing a working environment that was confusing and frustrating for everyone, and generating results that were mediocre at best, a disaster at worst. All of this is the result of failing to establish leadership as a professional practice, with foundational practices to be developed over time through experience.

"High performing leaders do not put spin of any kind on the truth."

Characteristics of high-performing, extraordinary leaders

High-performing leaders are different from amateurs in many ways. They do the work because it is worth doing, and view the work as their first priority and a commitment. They get things done *now*. Their priority is for improvement and excellence, never perfection in outcome, because they know that the quest for perfection is paralyzing. They work, regardless of the criticisms of others, to hone their leadership practice, and know that they will be prepared for the challenges when they come. They share power, rather than conserving it, knowing that sharing power extends their own power considerably. Such leaders do not put spin of any kind on the truth, neither glossing it over to avoid pain nor exaggerating concerns to "create a burning platform." They know that both approaches are manipulative, not authentic, and that leadership is not leadership without an ethical foundation. Such leaders are indifferent to both praise and blame. The opinions of others, unless being sought for improvement purposes, are irrelevant. When things get tough, they move forward, taking responsibility for their choices, even in the face of imperfect information. They know that, in a changing environment, there is always much contradiction and paradox, and that they must cultivate security and encourage risk-taking, creating passion for the new while letting go of the past.

They reject politics of all kinds, favoring authentic relationships instead. They offer trust and respect immediately, until it is betrayed, knowing that distrust just breeds more. They know that rigor and discipline are part of creativity and fun, measure what matters most (the outcomes), and give their best in all their work. Extraordinary leaders teach others to spread knowledge, learn from those around them, and aggressively seek others' input. To the master leader, failure does not exist. It is all learning. Resources are abundant, and their optimism in the face of challenges is contagious. In short, extraordinary leaders know that mental models (our thoughts) proscribe our reality, and that we must change the limits of our thoughts to create new and better reality.

What we know about emotion in the workplace

Extraordinary leaders understand that emotions in themselves are neither good nor bad, but a rich source for understanding how their people are responding to their leadership. Feelings bring focus to things that require attention. They are teachers impelling growth. Leaders can be so busy chasing process and technology that they lose sight of the fundamental purposes: people, with their hopes, fears, loves, and ambitions. You don't have to talk like an executive, spewing acronyms and mouthing obsession over financials, strategies and metrics. You only need to be human, connecting personally with those around you. The rest is mechanics. Some facts to consider:

Context counts. Where people are emotionally is affected by context, expectations, physical health, and other needs factors.

There are choices. Leaders manage attention on intention, using approaches anchored either in fear or in what is possible. People, all people, carry fear and doubt. Though they're usually not on display, they're there, usually for good reasons from past experience. We have all been bruised by others and have all inflicted bruises. Heartful leaders are resilient. They not only sustain the bruising but transform it into growth for themselves and others. When leaders foster an environment where people can face their doubts and fears to grow and self-realize, they achieve profound results. Instead of manipulating fear by conducting a "walk of shame," why not create a "walk of pride"? Most would want to be a part of that!

Extraordinary leaders know that mindful intention and emotional intention can work together. Why do people deal with the rational first, and then with the emotional? People are both, forever moving back and forth between these states. Perhaps due to training and other influences, leaders today seem obsessed with problems, and when they find them, they become obsessed with finding rational causes and solutions—before moving quickly to the next problem. This amateurish, obsessive approach sabotages learning, breeding blame instead of helping. (Remember, work is personal!) If truth be told, amateur leaders tend to value the rational, leaving emotions unresolved. However, feelings are one of the *gifts* human beings bring to their work, causing them to be more aware and tuned in. Perhaps it is time to listen, not only to the facts but to the emotions behind the facts. Perhaps people don't hear us and our intentions because we have not listened to them! Rational process without heart and spirit is not only misguided, it is corrosive, undermining the human spirit at the center of motivation. Perhaps, instead of merely solving problems, focus should be on listening to what matters most to people, and achieving both success and significance, feeding the inevitable appetite for more. Extraordinary leaders know that the logical thing to do is not necessarily the right thing to do, if emotions are in the way.

"Feelings are one of the gifts human beings bring to their work, causing them to be more aware and tuned in."

Extraordinary leaders act on intention! It is only when we act on our own vision and intentions that we begin realizing our passions. Action, and the risk that comes with it, comes first. Action sends a clear message that you mean what you say, and that your intentions are real. Without clear action to support intention, it all becomes nothing more than rhetoric, wishful thinking that's eventually seen as nothing more than a façade, not genuine leadership.

The leadership poisons

In working with many leaders, I've encountered some who have fallen victim to several "poisons" that contaminate their leadership effectiveness, even to the point of jeopardizing their careers. These poisons come in varying degrees, from the nuanced to the highly frontal, aggressive challenges to leadership practice. All are anchored in fear. While fear is a normal reaction to change and the resulting turmoil, it is a challenge—one that can either paralyze us or help us get focused on what matters most. Leadership, by definition, means working in an uncertain environment. Doubt, paradox, and confusion come with the job. When the challenges are not accepted and addressed, fear is a poison, with many forms.

Claiming victim status: Self-appointed victims are problematic wherever they show up in the organization, but when leaders take on a victim mentality, it is damaging to everyone around them. Such victimization manifests in a lot of ways, starting as a feeling that there is nothing the leader can do to affect certain situations. Budget and resource challenges, criticisms of staff and managers, pressure from other departments and many other concerns often leave leaders feeling helpless, cynical, and depressed. These folks seem to want to blame the world, or someone in it, for their problems, when in fact most are of their own making. When leaders allow this thinking into their leadership, they may think that they are using their "victimhood" as leverage to get something, but in reality, they are presenting themselves as having no power, undermining their own credibility with those they are leading. As long as we are dwelling obsessively on how we are being treated, the futility of our own efforts, or the lack of appreciation for our efforts, we are failing to do our work. Extraordinary leaders have no time for this, and know that there is always a way to move forward. And in the event that there is no way, they accept the situation and make the best of it in other ways while continuing to enlist mind, heart, and spirit in their work with their staff.

Failure to stand up to bullies: Bullies are everywhere, and do not operate on real power of their own. They are demanding, pushy, humiliating, and disrespectful. They use fear and anxiety to achieve compliance with their wishes. Bullies can be the leader's higher-ups, colleagues, and even direct reports. *They take their power from the fear of others.* But they inevitably back down when confronted by those who stand up to their bully behavior. Extraordinary leaders demonstrate both courage and self-respect! Bullying behavior is a significant test of a leader's right to lead, and backing down is abdication of that leadership responsibility, regardless of where it comes from. When you delay or postpone your intentions to deal with someone else's bullying demands, you allow their priorities to hijack your own.

A reluctance to decide: Many amateur leaders are guilty of the "ready/aim" syndrome. We are experts at talking ourselves out of acting, and the more training we've had, the better we are at it. It sounds like this: "Ready, aim... ready, aim... ready, aim. I'll fire when I am damn good and ready!" But they never fire, or do so too late. Hesitation is an enemy, often keeping us from doing the right thing. The single biggest reason people procrastinate: "We are not ready!" Bulls**t! This is fear talking, and it is persuasive, but wrong. Delaying decisions that must be made is about uncertainty and insecurity, plain and simple, and there will always be much that we do not know. When we hesitate to decide due to readiness,

"Leadership, by definition, means working in an uncertain environment. Doubt, paradox, and confusion come with the job."

65

politics, or myriad other excuses, we are giving our power to circumstances and others. Once input has been gathered and there is clarity about how the decision will be made, the leader with authority must decide. Information will always be imperfect; we'll never know for certain about the "rightness or wrongness" until we decide and act. This is an opportunity for the professional leader to exercise not only mind, but heart and spirit in making decisions. Wisdom means knowing what to do, and courage means doing it... now! Further, momentum requires that we start anything new before we are ready! The secret is to begin. Failure to do so is capitulation to fear. The extraordinary leader trusts informed intuition in situations like this.

Addictions: Were not talking here about addictions to drugs, alcohol, or other substances or undesired societal behaviors. We are talking here about addictions to factors in the work. Read this definition of addiction by the American Society of Addiction Medicine (https://www.asam.org/resources/definition-of-addiction):

> *"Addiction is a primary, chronic disease of brain reward, motivation, memory and related circuitry. Dysfunction in these circuits leads to characteristic biological, psychological, social and spiritual manifestations.... Addiction is characterized by inability to consistently abstain, impairment in behavioral control, craving, diminished recognition of significant problems with one's behaviors and interpersonal relationships, and a dysfunctional emotional response."*

Does it appear that "workaholism" meets these criteria? Think about what passes for "normal" leader behavior in many of today's organizations: obsession with metrics and standards, chasing of rewards and accolades, routine sacrifice of family and personal time for the sake of the business priorities, focus on money at the expense of meaning, creation of chaos and "burning platforms" to manipulate behaviors, etc. All of these behaviors result in heightened energy, and in the short term, produce results, leading to addiction behaviors anchored in "more is better." It is not! In the long term, people burn out, become resentful, and begin to act out in ways that are not healthy for the organization or for themselves. None of this is peaceful or normal!

Feeling that work needs to be enriching and fun (pain free) at all times. This is just plain delusional, and impedes growth of any kind. Pain is part of the professional performance cycle… things will go wrong, people will not always cooperate, there will always be politics and the system will break down. As Rassouli said (2016, p. 125), "New things don't happen when everything is perfect." It is never perfect! You will experience anxiety, frustration, and maybe even anger as you encounter challenge after challenge. Accept it, and get over it! Then get to work!

Extraordinary leaders never engage in or accept victim or bully behaviors from others who purport to be professionals, nor do they hesitate to make decisions or expect their work to be pain free. They seldom spend much time "fixing" others. Rather, they work to amplify what others bring as their strengths and talent.

Extraordinary leaders help others make their personal transformations— getting to breakthrough

High-performance leaders do not ignore their fears, but rise to the challenge of facing them in the work and do not make them the central focus of their decisions. They proceed with confidence, real confidence that only comes from knowing and owning who you are. They help people change themselves by coaching about what is expected, and why it is important. When you begin living and acting to realize your passion and intentions, you must be prepared for what you will find, and will inevitably create tension in relationships and even elicit criticism, envy, or even rejection. There will always be some in every work environment who struggle with understanding the

"Extraordinary leaders never engage in or accept victim or bully behaviors from others who purport to be professionals, nor do they hesitate to make decisions or expect their work to be pain free."

purposes, the work, or getting themselves engaged, and they may express their frustration through behaviors that are cynical, critical, and dismissive. Criticism and rejection are prerequisites for greatness! The temptation is to forego your passion. Don't! A "breakthrough" is in order. This is not a simple "Aha!" moment, where an employee suddenly understands something they had failed to comprehend before. Rather, this is a wholesale change in attitude and approach, without which the employee will fail. Breakthrough is a process with steps, listed here in a reasonably logical order, with the caveat that life sometimes is messier than this:

Step one: *Define both the organization's and the leader's intentions. Identify the opportunities, gifts, and competency gaps of the employee.* People are both the source of their problems and the solution to them. Conversation about this requires being firm and direct about their gifts and gaps. Such candor requires courage and resolve for the leader, but must occur if change is to take place.

Step two: *Change the environment and expectations, and redefine what is possible. You must disturb the peace!* This can be a little scary for people going through breakthrough. At this point, things start feeling a little strange, a little different, and unpredictable. It's a bit like driving into a new city with no map or GPS, and trying to find your way around without embarrassing yourself or, worse, getting lost. This is uncomfortable and unsettling. But it is a necessary part of the process.

Step three: *Challenge the discovery of new strength by stretching and expanding limits.* Begin experimentation by giving people "stretch" assignments, testing new limits. This "stretching" process will change thinking patterns, helping to create new habits and approaches to the work. It might even create a mess. But where is it written that everything needs to be neat and tidy? Perhaps the human creative process requires a bit of creative mess to keep things interesting. This is where change begins to anchor so that it can sustain.

Step four: *Pick a concrete goal, and expect—no, demand—action.* Action creates traction! Momentum counts as you help others change. Without action, there will be no change and therefore no new results. The leader must be present, in the moment, and able to tell the difference between what matters most and the mindless, egocentric chatter that comes from the competition for control. Focus on what matters most for those you coach. Insist that they take action.

Step five: *Map out the steps to a new future.* Through action and experience, people will change their understanding about who they are, what their work is, and how they go about doing it. This is an "inside job" and no one can do it for another. But you can help map it out using goals, action plans, approaches, etc. Without tenacity, anything done to create new approaches will be temporary at best, eroding as they reenter their familiar environments and daily actions.

Step six: *Establish and formalize new habits to build and sustain momentum.* This is the "lock- in" phase, where behavior repetition fosters habit and then habits become how things are done every day without a lot of conscious thought or deliberation. Breakthrough has occurred and is now who the person is, with no further need to reinforce or focus on it.

Breakthrough is most intense when driven from within, rather than imposed from outside. The best in-spirit leaders inspire people to live extraordinary lives of possibility and achievement. Obviously, it would be best to help people make their own breakthrough, but that is not always an option. It is sometimes necessary for the leader to firmly require significant change on the part of the individual, posing the risk of job jeopardy if that change does not occur. Look! Change will never stop... and everyone, including the leader, will have to change themselves if they want to thrive. In the end, there is no

"The best in-spirit leaders inspire people to live extraordinary lives of possibility and achievement."

such thing as disinteresting work or activity! Literally everything can bring value, learning, and energy. There are only disinterested people.

What leaders do to cultivate credibility among their followers

In summary, professional, high-performing leaders do very specific things to cultivate credibility as leaders among those they are there to lead. We will take further "deep dives" into some of these behaviors in later chapters, but some of the most significant ones are these:

1. They commit themselves to doing the leadership work, loving the work they do.

2. They are engaged, caring people who tend to seek opportunity, where others see only crisis or problems.

3. They take ego out of it, and do what matters most, right now and every day.

4. They are decisive, even and especially in the face of imperfect information. They move forward, integrating what they know from the data with what they know intuitively and experientially.

5. They assess risk because it is just plain smart, and never expect perfect information! There are no certainties and they know that life is riddled with paradox and ambiguity. They react to fear with the antidotes of courage and optimism.

6. They prioritize, and know that this *requires* de-selection. They know that decisions come with both cultural and emotional content. Purely rational decisions are usually insufficient. They understand that failure to decide cedes your power to others.

7. They have the courage and self-respect to reject victimization and stand up to bullies who do not respect them.

8. They tell the truth, and communicate what they know and intend with transparency, courage (take the risk that the truth will be

accepted and understood and assume the responsibility for its consequences), candor (say what you
see, no spin), and care (never blame, never shame,
and always offer respect, compassion, and understanding). This an essential function in learning
and making progress.

9. They never take praise or blame personally. It is
about the work and what matters most.

10. They measure outcomes, not steps. Outcomes are
what matters most.

11. Perfection is never the goal... improvement and
excellence are.

12. They are rigorous about doing the work, whether
or not they feel like it. They know that showing up
counts, that inspiration will follow, and to always
keep promises and take responsibility.

13. They share knowledge, skill, and power, and challenge others to become great.

14. They are willing to learn and to treat failure
as learning.

15. They know that not everyone will be inspired, and
may need help to move on.

16. They never allow fear to run their lives. Rather, they
know that fear and anxiety will never take them
where they want to go, and that they must allow
fear to move through them, and then act on intention with a healthy dose of enthusiasm if they are to
realize their intentions.

"They also understand that the fastest way to destroy engagement is to exert control."

Extraordinary leaders cultivate engagement

Amateurs leave engagement up to the employees, expecting them to bring their own emotional connection to the work with them. The intentional leader does not, instead taking the time to listen, understand, and support those who need support. Extraordinary leaders know that if they are not getting the results they want, it is up to them to change something. They also understand that the fastest way to destroy engagement is to exert control. The transcription staff at the beginning of this chapter vented their anger and then, with help to change their thoughts to more positive ideas about future possibility, began to prepare for their uncertain future. Transfer applications were completed, resumes were prepared, interview skills were practiced, and resources arrayed to help each employee find meaningful work, either in the organization, or outside of it. All eventually found placement, over a period of three months, and no one lost their job. When leaders demonstrate trust, confidence, honesty, and clarity, they are providing what people want most from them: respect. And over time, engagement will follow.

Two steps on the path to cultivating a professional leadership mindset

Extraordinary leaders integrate mind, heart, and spirit in their practice of leadership. They are fully committed, get things done, and treat people with high regard, challenging and helping them perform at levels that they did not know they could. As you reflect on the messages in this chapter, consider how this applies to your leadership by answering the questions in Step 1, and by taking the action challenges in Step 2. Take time to reflect, listen internally to what matters most to you, and journal your what you are learning.

Step 1:

> » What is your level of commitment to your purposes? And to your organization?

> » What three specific things have you done to inspire those around you?

» Have you identified any self-appointed victims and bullies? What are you doing to address the issues they create?

» What specific promises have you made to those around you about your leadership? What are you doing to keep those promises?

Step 2:

» Identify specific significant changes in your work, and publicly commit to making them.

» Confront one self-appointed victim about what they are doing, and what they need to do to change, and the consequences if they do not.

» Confront one bully in your work/life and make it clear how they must treat you and others from this time forward, and the consequences if that does not occur.

» Identify one potential "star," and coach that person to succeed at something they've never done before.

"Extraordinary leaders integrate mind, heart, and spirit in their practice of leadership."

PART 2:
Making It Happen—
Putting Foundations to Work

"Purpose is not ready-made; it must be shaped
and clarified through our acting on it."
—Leider, R. 2004, p.35

Today, we live in a world that Dr. Judith Orloff describes (Orloff, 2009, p. 1) as "a pressure cooker society that pushes us to our emotional limits." Among many factors, there is an increasing expectation of perfection, and a growing tendency to depersonalize work. There seems to be an art to making life more difficult and complicated than it needs to be. But extraordinary leaders move away from the complicated toward the simple, and attend to the whole person (mind, heart, spirit). They also act decisively, often with imperfect information. Making things happen is like preparing breakfast: break the egg, cook it, then eat it. Getting ready to act, or trying to act, is not acting. It is planning and organizing, and nothing of real substance occurs. There is no "try" in any of that. Practice means real action. Leadership theory without consequent action is self-indulgent nonsense! "I will try to improve" is an excuse to fail, right from the beginning, making everything more complicated in the consequent efforts "to try."

Part 2 is less about the "what" and more about the "how." Most people ask: "What can I do to make my situation serve my needs?" Extraordinary leaders ask more and different questions: "How can I meet the needs that are present in my situation? Do I own the room?" So, ask yourself: are you a leader in your very presence, making things happen to meet needs that arise, regardless of titles or labels? Do you respect others in the process, and respect the power you have in achieving your purposes? When you do, you have found your authentic self as a leader.

CHAPTER 6

Respecting Self—
Do You Own the Room?

"We need a certain amount of consistency—a degree of predictability—
in our personalities, so that we can function effectively in the world
as trustworthy human beings."
—Peck, p. 24

KEY POINTS SUMMARY

» Do you "own the room"? The leader must take responsibility for creating conditions for engagement in the workplace.

» Extraordinary leaders do things differently than others.

» Fostering loyalty is an emotional process and will take time. If people are really "assets," treat them with loyalty.

» Master leaders make promises, keep them, and ensure that boundaries are clear.

» Politics are poison, undermining trust, a prime requirement for engagement.

» Eliminate ambiguity and provide clarity about responsibilities, accountabilities, and what is acceptable.

Owning the room

Shelly met me for dinner in advance of an improvement process that I would be supporting as her coach/consultant. My purpose was to understand the people involved in the three-day event, and to make sure Shelly knew her role as team leader for it. She arrived nervous and embarrassed, revealing that she was intimidated by two of the participants (both of whom reported to her) because they were "lean-trained facilitators," and took full charge of most meetings they were involved in, a role she felt was inappropriate. But she did not know how to respond to this, other than to defer to their training. As we talked, her CEO joined us, listened in, and then asked her a question: "Do you own the room?" Confused, she asked what he meant. "Shelly," he said, "I did not appoint them to lead this project, I appointed you. It is yours to own, and if you don't, others will fill the vacuum. Own the room, and make it clear that the final decisions are yours. They need this from you. They are trained facilitators, not trained leaders." The next morning, Shelly entered the meeting with confidence and self-respect. She spelled out the agenda, individual roles and responsibilities, and the decisional processes the group would use, including that, in the absence of group agreement, she would be the deciding presence. Her confidence was profound, and she commanded everybody's attention. The need for a calm, confident tenacity cannot be overstated. Leaders must take the reality that presents itself, and orchestrate everything possible to make the most of it. But it is not just about what you do… it is about who you are. Do you respect yourself as a leader?

Extraordinary leaders are different

Much daily discourse about leadership tends to be simplistic at best, and degrading at worst, via gossip and opinionating. Recent popular literature obsesses over a small sample research report (261 American CEOs) out of Australia's Bond University, suggesting that one of five CEOs have traits like those of psychopaths and prisoners, more than the population at large (www. telegraph.com.uk/news/2016/09/13). An earlier study found the number to be one of twenty-five, not exactly consistency of findings across several studies. (www.patheos.com/blogs/drishtikone/2013/10). What is unstated is that results are similar for entrepreneurs, researchers, and educators. I admit that I have met and experienced the misery of working for one or two such characters, but in a forty-five-year career with well over 500 CEOs in my experience, I suspect I would have met more than a couple if this research were valid. Maybe I am just doing a great job picking my clients and colleagues! Perhaps there is more going on here than what is being reported. (Good grief! Let's assume that most leaders are not primarily narcissists and psychopaths!)

However, many in leadership today think that leadership must include some form of "bravery," usually expressed as a bit of assertive/aggressive presence in the face of issues and difficulties. Bravado statements like "We must drive improvement!" or "Get on the train, or get off!" or even "We must create a burning platform!" are all testosterone-laden declarations that sound somehow courageous. But none is. Unfortunately, this kind of bravery often gets you into trouble, but doesn't necessarily get you out. We can decide to do something out of the ordinary, maybe even something that is very controversial, but the real test is whether we can sustain our decision in the aftermath. That calls for courage, competence, skill, and very good relationships with those who are doing the daily work. Courage requires that we step outside of our comfort zone, and risk criticism, ridicule, and even rejection in an environment that is never static, always changing and flowing. Such courage is the result of achievement over time. We don't practice leadership in short bursts then return to some "non-leader" state. We are leaders in every moment, in every thought and action. As a leader, whether you like or dislike a circumstance is irrelevant. The big question is: "what will you do?"

"Courage requires that we step outside of our comfort zone, and risk criticism, ridicule, and even rejection in an environment that is never static, always changing and flowing."

The defining element in assuming leadership responsibility is the quality of the relationship leaders have with employees. Some believe that their rituals, procedures, rules, and policies are real and necessary. They create teams, write plans, map processes, do experiments, and lock in change with policy and standard work. But in the face of over-facilitated, consensus-based problem-solving like this, people sometimes just want to shake the leader and demand to be told what to do. Change is hard… we know how to do the old dance, and that's the dance we want to do. But nothing is permanent, none of it will last. What lasts is the capacity for conversation that transforms relationships. At the highest levels of mastery, leaders see that what they are engaged in has little to do with specific daily tasks, outcomes, or reward, and everything to do with the quality of relationships. This requires new dance steps. To blindly follow the rules and processes without question is to give over control to others who have learned new ways. Those who are willing to learn know that the best leaders are open to everything but attached to nothing. However, that requires aggressive listening. Do we listen to people to respond? Or do we listen to hear and understand who they are and what they intend?

People need to know on a personal level who their leaders are, and to trust that those leaders have their interests in mind as they make the decisions required to ensure business success. This requires that leaders know themselves well, first. As leaders, "we are participants, not observers. Accepting this means taking responsibility for ourselves" (Issacs, p.124). We, and no one else, own the quality of our relationships. Each of us is largely in control of our own life. Who we are and what we do are the accumulation of many choices, some good and some not. Extraordinary leaders are driven to "go beyond," to excel beyond where they are today. To them, limitations present themselves as challenges, never boundaries. While this can be unsettling for some, it is energizing for others, and the master leader understands how to exercise that energy.

Unfortunately, too often, an "us versus them" mindset exists, pitting leaders against employees and departments against departments, with everyone wondering why the environment is so negative. People often get caught up in their own internal melodramas—us/them, good/bad, right/wrong. Such polarized environments are emotional, filled with gossip, petty disputes and anxiety, yet amateur leaders attempt to attack the issues with rational solutions. Ponder this: you cannot resolve emotional issues with rational solutions. **(Read that last sentence three times!)** The centered leader observes this quietly, and then decides on the next response calmly and assertively. An environment of engagement requires an environment of emotional connection in relationships. Do you have the courage to deal with your own anxieties and mistrust rather than trying to blame and change everyone else? It is precisely at those times when our lives seem in chaos that we feel most alone and isolated from others. Reaching out is the beginning of reestablishing order and reconnecting with others. The implications are profound. If you want engagement, you must connect authentically and emotionally and take responsibility for everything that presents itself. Own the room!

"Ponder this: you cannot resolve emotional issues with rational solutions."

What about loyalty?

When leaders "own the room" and cultivate strong positive relationships with staff, the resulting "frame of relationships" sets the stage for loyalty. Loyalty is not a word often heard today in business. It evokes a response more cynical than positive. Increasingly, people find it difficult to entrust leaders with their job security, investments, and futures. The Pew Research Center, in 2011, published data (Pew Research Center, March 11-21 Q18a-n) showing that more than 50 percent of us hold negative views of banks, financial institutions, congress, government, large corporations, labor unions, and the entertainment industry. Those that rated higher than 50 percent (but not much higher) in trustworthiness included colleges and universities, churches, small businesses, and technology companies.

Too often, leaders describe loyalty as something they expect of others, even demand. One of the worst things a leader can do is attempt to force loyalty from people who have not decided to be loyal to them. Loyalty must be earned. How can an organization expect loyalty from staff if leaders are not willing to be loyal to them? (Think lay-offs, downsizing, etc.) It is easy to rationalize the breaking of promises. What is difficult is rebuilding trust in the aftermath. Knowingly deciding to do the wrong thing is giving yourself permission to be irresponsible. Do we keep our commitments to ourselves as well as those we make to others?

Loyalty decisions others make are not the leader's affair. People already want to belong, and will choose to be committed to something bigger than themselves. Most people experience motivation as a form of restlessness, tension created by the gap between what they have and what they want. In fact, despite all of our efforts to control behavior through policy and environment, the truth is that people are still going to do pretty much what they damn well please! The extraordinary leader views this gap as oppor-tunity to grow, achieve, and succeed, and encourages this opportunity by offering loyalty in return for the emotional energy required for organization success. They know people will give their loyalty to those who are loyal to them. Of course, in return for a loyalty commitment, the organization has the *right* to expect dedication, high performance, and continuous learning. Ultimately, life is less about what we know and feel and more about who we are. Your followers will make their own decisions about loyalty.

The centered leader

In today's consumer mindset, we tend to think that more is better, and that if a little of something is good, then a lot is even better! (Think chocolate, wine, any food, etc.) This mindset can lead to greed and even addiction, both of which destroy success. Authentic leaders are centered and focus on what they have, inspired to reach their goals. They spend little time or attention on things they don't have or want. More is not necessarily better. Some of this is intuitive, and centered leaders rely on their intuition as much as facts and data. Our five physical senses (data) require that we pay attention to what is going on outside ourselves. But there are other non-physical "senses" we can employ: our intuition and sense of humor, to name two. Intuition requires that we pay attention to what is going on inside, and centered leaders have, through experience, come to trust their intuition, their inner knowing, so much that they feel little need to explain themselves or their decisions to others. Rather, they focus on just being themselves. To achieve this, sometimes leaders must remove themselves from the barrage of demands, requests, and other distracting noises that keep them from tending to their own internal vision, which others often cannot see. Sometimes you have to allow things to get pretty messy for a while before you can make progress. This means slowing down, having a sense of humor about the mess, and even full withdrawal from the situation sometimes, allowing the mess, particularly during times of rapid, robust change. When change starts to spiral toward chaos, the extraordinary leader's path is often counter-intuitive to most of those around them. The old ways no longer work, but most want to stay on the old, familiar path. In our "more is better" obsession, we are rewarded for "yes" and punished for "no." This inevitably leads to multiple number-one priorities, lack of focus, and wasted time on the trivial.

But the leader must carve a new path, with thoughtful and firm resolve, which can be both frightening and painful for many. Authentic leaders know that such discomfort is not to be avoided, that doing so would mean that pain and fear run their lives. "No" is a complete sentence, and must be stated when people refuse to change. If you do not set the priorities in your life and work, others will do

"Despite all of our efforts to control behavior through policy and environment, the truth is that people are still going to do pretty much what they damn well please!"

so gladly. The best leaders know that before integrating a new reality, you must first experience dis-integration. This is not optional.

Extraordinary leaders, in this context, seldom worry about reputation or security. They understand that reputation has little to do with themselves. Rather, it is promoted by the judgments and criticisms of others, who often have their own agendas. You can't reach your goals by wasting time and energy being validated or offended by others, whether well-intentioned or not. Leaders pay little attention to others' judgment. Those who judge are merely defining themselves. What others think about you is their business, not yours! As long as you are trying to please others, you cannot breathe freely, relax into your role, and offer authentic leadership. Feedback tends to push us in the directions *others* see as best for us and them. Never accept any arbitrary criticism or judgment from another, no matter who! This includes your own "self-talk"! We all have an inner judge, an inner wimp, and an inner observer. The judge is always critical, the wimp is overly concerned about safety and comfort, the observer only reports facts, without taking a position. All of them are liars, keeping you from your dreams.

Centered leaders stay focused on their own intentions, and leave their reputation to others. Worrying about security only makes you more insecure, and does little to improve or cultivate confidence in self or others. It is a poor approach for growth, innovation, and accomplishment. Self-reliance and personal accountability are at the heart of lasting personal power. Without either attribute, victimization drives behavior, with people waiting for others to satisfy their wants and needs.

Leaders must be careful about their own emotions when leading others and making decisions. When taking risks and acting to move forward, the wise understand that you don't always land where you intend. Fear, anger, loss, and suffering are never great platforms for effective decisions. But they do present us with an important personal choice: enslavement to our emotional state, or the opportunity to exercise courage and the discipline to be who we aspire to be. It is useful, even necessary, to sometimes just relax the tension. Relaxing is not lazy. It is recharging, so that new energy and new ideas can simmer.

Extraordinary leaders build trust and end politics

Creating an engaged environment requires trusting relationships and a refusal to play politics. Let's consider both:

Trusting relationships foster engagement. Without trust, there will be little interchange, self-disclosure, or willingness to risk time, energy, and effort in doing something new, different, or a stretch. Trust is there when people make promises and keep them, do what they say they're going to do, and finish what they start. This includes big things and small, like showing up on time for work or meetings (small), or completing a major project on time, within budget, and with all goals met (big). There is no such thing as a "small" promise. Failure to keep promises, big or small, teaches others we are not reliable. Trust relationships, however, are often fouled up in some pretty nuanced ways. Bullying bosses, broken promises, and truth spinning undermine trust. Due to anxiety, amateur leaders sometimes micro-manage the results, creating a sense of distrust in the very professionals hired to do the work, inadvertently sending the message that they don't have confidence staff will get the job done. Amateur leaders sometimes invite people to offer input on the work, but have a "hidden" desire to convince these people about the solutions they've already decided on. These practices are a form of bullying, and they undermine trust and therefore staff engagement. "When a leader trusts no one, no one trusts him" (Tao, 17th verse, as cited in Dyer, 2007, p. 76). Why would anyone hire people with special knowledge if they were going to question and manage every decision made and every step taken?

It's very simple to test whether you have a trust relationship with your staff: ask them to describe the progress

> "The best leaders know that before integrating a new reality, you must first experience dis-integration. This is not optional."

they've made in their life or work, the challenges they've encountered, and the frustrations they've experienced, and see how they respond. If they respond openly, with energy and directly, it's likely there is trust. If they dance, couch their words, or redirect, avoiding mention of the challenges and frustrations, trust is likely not there. It may be time to re-examine the relationship and your role in it. Have promises been broken? Has information been withheld? Has help been denied? People are more than skilled machines doing their jobs. They are relating creatures and willing to trust one another if conditions are right. They want to be responsible and to help, but they need to be sure their honesty will be treated with respect and care. It is the professional leader's job to cultivate a sense of trust and ownership of the work.

The refusal to "play politics" is also important in building an engaged workplace. Politics are about power and influence, usually generating a win/lose mindset among those who participate. Often, they are designed *deliberately* to spin facts, obscure truth, and convince (manipulate) people to do things they would otherwise not want to, using approaches that are often less than honest. Even explaining and convincing, commonly thought of as negotiating processes, are forms of control that fit into the definition of politics. Behaving this way is actually attempting to *control* perceptions and actions of others, but few will eagerly sign up to be controlled by others. "Spinning" the truth with a win/lose mentality, done often in today's political and business environments, is by its very nature dishonest and destructive, undermining trust and goodwill. Who, after all, wants to be "spun"?

The extraordinary leader's success does not depend on winning with lies or someone else failing! The reverse is actually true. Honest success breeds success in others, producing even more success. This requires speaking the truth, no spin. While sometimes painful, the truth can always be a source of healing, energy, and goodwill. Leaders never submit to those who bully or intimidate, or allow any outside force to cause them to deny what they know to be truth. Nor do they expect others to do so. The best leaders trust in their own experience or worldview, cultivate their own individuality and that of others, and proceed toward the extraordinary, rather than what is common. They surround themselves with people who bring their own joy and resolve with them to the work, and help those who do not have that joy find it.

My "List of Nevers"!

It is important, as we do the work of leadership, that we consider boundaries. I've developed in my work a "list of nevers" that articulate my boundaries as a leader. I offer them as an example only... every leader should have their own such list, developed from experience and learning over an entire career:

» Never allow the circumstances or appearances in the moment discourage you from your purpose. Rather, treat them as beacons, leading you to your next beginning.

» Never accept any arbitrary criticism or judgment from another, no matter who.

» Never spend a nickel on someone who does not have your or the organization's interests in mind. Some do not belong where they are, and must be removed.

» Never give self-proclaimed victims power! They will just become tyrants (more on this later!).

» Never get caught in the web of shame and blame spun by others.

» Never ask for "buy-in" when you mean compliance. It's dishonest and creates cynicism. If you want buy-in, encourage co-authorship.

» Never use thoughtless process as a replacement for relational wisdom.

» Never allow teamwork to become a substitute for or abdication of personal responsibility.

"The best leaders trust in their own experience or worldview, cultivate their own individuality and that of others, and proceed toward the extraordinary, rather than what is common."

» If appointments are more than fifteen minutes late, don't do business. And if calls aren't returned, do not call again.

» Never believe that you can be "friends" with someone who works for you (friendly, yes; friends, no). You may have to let that "friend" go someday for performance.

» Never ask others what they think of your decisions once they are made. Trust your own intuition and judgment.

» Never make excuses for someone who is failing. They own the failure, and you need to keep ownership of that where it belongs.

» Never judge a person based on the opinions of others. Judgment is the antithesis of peace, creating tension, anxiety, and resentment.

» Never compromise the compromise. If an agreement is reached and promises are made, keep them, no exceptions, or you will never have trust.

» Never allow self-appointed victims, liars, or charlatans to affect your life.

All of these "Nevers" are pointed at those individuals who, at a profound level, truly do not want to engage in the work or with the organization that hired them, those that I call "the disengaged." By definition, disengaged people do not want to be there, and have no plans to leave. This must be dealt with. Not everyone can be won over, nor will everyone be willing to engage in the work (more on this in Chapter 8). After much effort on your part to bring about change, you may find it necessary to relieve those individuals from their duties, so that the organization can move on. When that becomes necessary, act with respect for the individual at all times, with the intention that you are helping them be successful... somewhere else. This is a legitimate and serious leadership function. Failure to act will breed cynicism and erode the engagement of others, causing the failure of the organization to perform well on its intentions.

Leadership is not about the process, but about who "owns the room"!

In our improvement work, some are often quick to say that "problem-solving is about the process, not the people." They are trying to convey that the problems being solved and resulting improvements are not the fault of the people doing the work, and that is usually true. But leadership is all about the people, not the process. Solely focusing on the process first means failure. People do not come to work just to work. They want to be seen, to be recognized, to be acknowledged, to be valued. It is people who do the work, not some sterile process that all are compelled by "standard work" to follow. It is people who provide the resources. It is people who assess the success or failure of what is done. It is people who learn and grow over time.

Our battle as leaders is more within ourselves than with others. We must own what we are saying and doing. Leaders must "own" the processes and functions, and the conditions involved in getting work done through the people in their charge, much like Shelly at the beginning of this chapter had to take ownership of the improvement process she was responsible for leading. Growth as a professional leader requires that you abandon security, say yes to possibility, and allow yourself to take risks that will enable you to become more than you are today. This means a healthy sense of self-reliance and personal accountability. As a professional, if you want more freedom, you must create more value. As an extraordinary leader, you must make a difference! "Own the room" by taking these responsibilities as your own and you will have taken the first step in building true, authentic, emotional connection with your staff, and they with their work.

"By definition, disengaged people do not want to be there, and have no plans to leave. This must be dealt with."

Two steps on the path to cultivating respect for self—owning the room

Extraordinary leaders know themselves and cultivate loyalty through positive relationships, building trust, and ending politics. They "own the room." As you reflect on the messages in this chapter, consider how this applies to your leadership by answering the questions in Step 1 and taking the challenges in Step 2. Take time to reflect, listen internally to what matters most to you, and journal what you are learning as you do this.

Step 1:

» What three things about your leadership make you "come alive"?

» What is your level of commitment to your purposes? And to your organization?

» Do you know who you are without titles and labels?

» What are you doing to cultivate a climate of loyalty and high performance?

» What are you doing to eliminate politics in favor of authentic relationships and expectations?

Step 2:

» Find two opportunities to "own the room" and assert your leadership in a kind but definitive way.

» Confront two people who you feel have shown disrespect in the past. Set new boundaries.

CHAPTER 7

Respecting Others— So, Why Do People Do the Work They Do?

"Man's search for meaning is the primary motivation in his life."
—Viktor Frankl, p. 105

KEY POINTS SUMMARY

» The leader's job is to create an environment that enables personal transformation and growth. This is both rational and emotional work.

» Engagement cannot be forced on people. It occurs when conditions are right, and people choose to engage.

» People are emotional creatures, and emotion is a gift, not an obstacle. We cannot resolve emotional issues/problems with rational solutions.

» Most reward systems are, at the core, bullying and manipulative, breeding cynicism and resentment rather than motivation and engagement. Bully behavior produces short-term results, but at great long-term expense.

» The desire to grow and develop is hardwired into us. We are all able to transform ourselves.

Strolling into the large conference room, my intuitive radar signaled what could only be described as "icy." Two executives, the COO and a VP of operations, were co-leading a meeting of their managers, with the VP at the flipchart. Managers were expressing concerns about their workload, the burnout they were feeling, and their worries that supervisors and staff were feeling the same. These folks were unloading! From the back of the room, I noted the visible pain on the faces of many of the managers. The meeting was not going well. Suddenly, the lean-trained VP of operations held a marker up, declaring, "Let's root-cause our feelings about all of this!" The entire room went cold, in dead silence. The now confused COO tried to elicit reasons for their feelings, but nobody was having any of it. The silence persisted. Clear to everyone but the two executives? There was simply too much to do. What was there to "root-cause"? And clearly, to me at least, the executives did not own the room.

Frustrated, the COO signaled me to help, and gladly invited me to the front, where I quietly told the group that I respected their feelings, wanted them to resume explaining how they were feeling, and that I would listen until we had a full understanding of all of it, no charting and no notes. The conversation immediately exploded, with people voicing their candid concerns and allowing answers to several heartfelt questions. We even made a few on-the-spot staffing decisions, and resolved to come together in a week to update and continue. The managers left feeling heard.

When others are in emotional stress or pain, the very worst thing you can do is deny it, dismiss it, or attempt to problem-solve it away. All are forms of control, and lead to resistance and more disorder. Intent listening is not a communication skill! It is being present. When we are not present to those around us (focused on outcomes, distractions, cell phones, etc.), we lose power. Being present, paying attention, is living life consciously. The last thing we want to do is silence those who disagree, or those who are in pain. Doing so only drives distress deeper, amplifying the hurt and even provoking an attack. Sometimes, the most powerful thing an executive can do in such a situation is nothing at all. Leaders must have the courage to engage in relationships *emotionally* to support the people around them. People can and will heal themselves, without a leader's "solutions." What they most want is to be heard. Face the emotion, and acknowledge it. Do leaders have the courage to stay with the conversation long enough to understand, and to forge a higher-state relationship with those they lead?

Most leaders today favor the rational first

Some leaders work very hard to control everything about them. They are operating out of fear and a sense of inadequacy. Many leadership texts assume that logic rules and things must be coherent. The idea is to plan, organize, and control. The leader should be able to see cause and effect, and should be able to identify a problem, root-cause it, enact the right solution to solve it, and then standardize behaviors to sustain results. The executives in the situation above were well trained in that process, but in the world of human beings, things aren't quite that clean.

While people are rational creatures, they are also emotional and spiritual creatures, complete with both inspiration and doubt. It is the wonderful integration of these human aspects that define humanity. Relying on the rational at the expense of heart and spirit produces leadership that is sterile, impersonal, and insensitive to what is really happening. Such leadership is amateur in understanding human drives, and pays little attention to the needs and wants of others unless those needs and wants serve their own goals as well. Standardizing and controlling work will definitely improve productivity and perhaps quality. But over time, it also depletes creativity, the joy of discovery, and human energy, replacing it with boredom and often apathy. Taken too far, standardization leads to perfectionism, a counter-productive response to inner doubt. Such doubt is a negative energy rooted in fear that undermines relationships and destroys self-confidence, as

"When others are in emotional stress or pain, the very worst thing you can do is deny it, dismiss it, or attempt to problem-solve it away."

well as trust. This negative energy is neither gentle nor forgiving, logical but never inspirational. It doesn't matter to the rational mind how hard you try, what matters are results! This creates a dynamic that discourages any sign of "weakness," as if asking for help and stating your truth is weakness. It is not!

Our emotional side, however, wants to believe that trying should be recognized as evidence of your engagement and willingness to help. The spiritual side may go even further, insisting that trying is the only thing that matters, as the ultimate source of meaning, energy, and enthusiasm for a higher purpose. These different pulls can sometimes create significant tension, causing internal confusion and distress. When this tension plays out in groups of people, polarization can become quite pronounced. People often get caught up in their own melodramas: us/them, good/bad, right/wrong, all of which undermines trust and the ability to work together on what matters most, killing the possibility for any innovation and self-direction in favor of security. When trust in one another is absent, the result is often disrespect for others, loneliness, alienation, and sometimes even cruelty. Key to navigating such tension in the work is a profound understanding of the environment required for strong engagement, and knowledge required to foster more engaging relationships. The centered leader observes the tensions quietly, and decides on the next response calmly and assertively. Instead of making someone wrong, the extraordinary leader will find a way to join those who disagree in dialogue that makes all parties right. Above all, extraordinary leaders never give up their aspirations, but rather give up their anxieties, limited-resource mindsets, and self-criticism.

Why do people work?

People work for many reasons, including survival, power, approval, and accomplishment. But beyond everything else, most seek meaning and purpose. When stressed, our instincts are for self-preservation. What we do for that purpose can usually be labeled as fear, and often results in holding onto the "old ways" that are certain, instead of exploring new ones. This is not good and is possibly dangerous in a changing environment. Unfortunately, not everyone understands or believes this.

Dr. Richard Pierson sat across the table, smiling con-
genially as we discussed a recent employee survey that
described him as arrogant and often sarcastic in his
treatment of coworkers. His behavior was cited by staff
as a major cause of decline in morale over the previous
two years. Dr. Pierson's response to the feedback was
unusual. He *agreed* with everything in the report. Instead
of excuses, explanations or any kind of regret, he beamed:
"Of course I use sarcasm to motivate my team. It works!"
When informed that there are no credible motivational
models that encourage the use of sarcasm, his response was
unwavering. "Sarcasm works for me, and I am not about
to change how I lead because of feedback in a survey!"

Unfortunately, Dr. Pierson is not alone in his use of
sarcasm and belittlement in the pursuit of compliance
and business outcomes. Some leaders hold cultural beliefs
that are simply not good, even poisonous at times—racial
and gender bias, intolerance and victimization, to name
a few. Shaming and blaming are considered normal in
many environments. When things are not going as we
want, the default position seems to be that the problem
rests with other people. Yet the truth is likely that the
problem, or at least some of it, lies within ourselves. One
CEO/author describes what he calls the "walk of shame,"
publicly berating people for their mistakes and waste in
their work, as his way of getting them to pay attention.
Good grief: it requires little intelligence to criticize the
work of others, tear them down and make them feel
the weight of all their errors and flaws. Generations of
research shows that such punishment *demotivates* rather
than motivates. It is time to call blaming and shaming
what they are… negativity. Some such leaders claim that
they are just being "realists," but they are not… they are
negative, and disrespectful! You can't lead from spirit if
you blame and shame others for what is occurring. Why

*"Instead
of making
someone
wrong, the
extraordinary
leader will
find a way
to join those
who disagree
in dialogue
that makes all
parties right."*

would anyone demean or even abuse others to get things done? Judgment and harmony cannot co-exist. People are attracted to and energized by positive reinforcement, not negative. Belittling and berating others keeps you in your lower energies, bogging you down and straining your emotions. Such blame is a form of distraction from the discomfort that comes with realizing your own responsibility when things do not work as planned. Using fear to motivate merely creates resentment and cynicism, and does nothing to move you forward. When we shame others, we are telling them that they are somehow unworthy of our respect. Such judgment leads to isolation. If you want your work to accomplish real purpose, you must let go of any desire to create melodrama. It just distracts and demoralizes those who are there to help you. What requires intelligence and imagination is the ability to inspire people to stretch, learn, and grow. Extraordinary leaders never give up on the possibilities that people bring. Such leaders are first in offering respect, knowing that one cannot have respect of the other without doing so. Self-awareness and reflection can help you avoid being dragged into negative thinking.

For too long, focus has been on the wrong questions

Extraordinary leadership is not a goal, it is a way of being, of acting. A desire for excellence and achievement is supported by knowledge and skill, but only as a baseline of competence. Excellence is more about personal energy and attitude, an unwillingness to do anything but your very best, and an expectation that others will do so as well. So, we ask what we think are the obvious questions: "How do I motivate people to do their very best? How do I get them to buy in? How I get people to be more engaged? Should I use incentives to cause (bribe?) people to do what needs to be done? What are the best incentives? Does money motivate? How can I keep my employees happy?" Scott Peck answered that last question (Peck, pp. 32/33): "The biggest lie promoted by various of our social institutions—and this in some ways plays into our human nature and our sin of laziness—is at work here, to be happy all the time... the truth is that our finest moments, more often than not, occur precisely when we are uncomfortable, when we're not feeling happy or fulfilled, when we're struggling and searching."

In other words, trying to make people happy, or engaged, may not be a worthy goal that leads to excellence. No one, not even the best of leaders, can tell a person what they must do to make themselves happy. This is a solo journey, without a clear map or GPS to guide the process.

Some complain that people today are not motivated like they were "in the old days." While this is a sentimental perspective, looking through the lens of the past will only keep you in the past. It will never take you to your future. Actually, complaints come from looking at the past. Inspiration comes from looking forward… you choose: sentimental attachment to the past, or inspiration about what is possible in the future!

In reality, motivation is just as strong and intense in the human creature as it's always been. Try conducting a very simple test. Communicate to a few people that there is free pizza in the lunchroom. (Make sure there *is* free pizza in the lunchroom, first!) In minutes, you will have moved many toward the lunchroom, all of their own free will. (By the way, another interesting facet of this little test is *that communication does not seem to be a problem either*. It seems that everyone gets the message, even when mumbled or garbled in some way.) People are intrinsically motivated, and want to do the right thing, as long as the right thing is fairly easy to do, and especially if it serves their self-interests. The real question is: are they motivated to accomplish the intentions of the organization in the same spirit, and have we made it easy to do, and in their self-interest? If not, then motivational alignment has not occurred—a leadership problem, not a staff problem.

When people lose interest in the work, it may be that the leader has lost interest in the people doing the work. It is a choice to accept aging, atrophying, and obsolescence. It may be that, in our obsession with defining and solving

"No one, not even the best of leaders, can tell a person what they must do to make themselves happy. This is a solo journey, without a clear map or GPS to guide the process."

problems, we have perhaps forgotten how to savor the moment and live effectively in the present. One of the most difficult realities of leadership is recognizing that you are not in charge of the path people are on. The more you try to control people, manage events, and drive results, the sooner you find yourself frustrated and disappointed.

Maybe better questions are in order

How do we relate to the people we are leading? Are they co-authors of our common destiny, or merely there to serve our needs? We must choose, and in doing so, chart the path to the future. A number of very important studies over the past few years posed the question, "Are people engaged, and what motivates them?" These rigorous studies have been conducted by Gallup, SHRM, Hewitt, the Conference Board, and other organizations, as hard science, with consistent findings about which factors motivate. Key elements of engagement that emerge from this work include clarity of intention (I know what we are trying to do, and my role in it), and focus on possibility, vision, and hope (We can make a better world), both touched on earlier. In addition, the studies suggest two other elements requiring our attention: The willingness to "own" the important work that must be done (I will offer my input) and a positive relationship with leadership (I am recognized as important and adding value). A meta-analysis of surveys done involving over 1.4 million employees by Gallup showed a 22 percent higher level of productivity in organizations reporting higher levels of engagement (Baldoni, J., HBR, July 4, 2013). Engagement pays off in business performance.

There is tension in every workplace, arising from the gap between goals and current state, cost and revenue, standardization and personal autonomy. People bring gifts and capabilities, and can work together to channel that tension in useful, productive ways, as a source of energy! Engagement occurs when we allow people, at a genuine level, to influence us, and we them. This is the test of an authentic leadership, outweighing any other challenge. You cannot force people to engage in the work, but you can invite them into your improvement efforts to help themselves. There are better questions than those posed earlier: "What can this person on my staff do uncommonly well?" Or "How can we organize to help one another, rather than organizing merely for personal convenience and efficiency?" If we ask better questions, we can encourage movement based on emotional energy rather than simply based on reason, and emotions are contagious.

"You cannot force people to engage in the work, but you can invite them into your improvement efforts to help themselves."

It takes clarity and resolve for the leader to detach from reason, and enlist the emotions of others. Leaders seeking more energy and staff engagement must begin with actions that help those staff, and appeal to them emotionally. This means paying attention to the conditions that foster engagement, and getting on with it! In leadership, we seldom "find" meaning. Rather, we *make* meaning through choice and action.

What we know about motivation

Due to much research done in the twentieth century, we know a lot about why people do what they do. Through the work of Maslow, MacGregor, Herzberg, Blake and Mouton, Bennis, et al., we understand the needs and wants that tend to affect human behavior and performance. There are some basic principles:

At a basic level, people are volunteers in the workplace. As adults, people make their own decisions. They choose their professions, choose to apply for a job, choose to take it when offered, and choose to stay over time. Extraordinary leaders know that you cannot make someone invest in themselves or inspire themselves... only they can do that, and it is a solo act. Such volunteerism requires respect and acknowledgment. Good leaders know how to ask for what they want. (If you have children, you know that most kids seem to have this skill, but we seem to lose it as adults.) Most people want to help, to please, and to be involved. So, ask them to do so!

Context counts. Where people are motivationally at any given moment depends on expectations, physical health, and other individual need factors that influence how they think and feel in that moment. Respect context and the challenges that ensue.

People will choose pride over fear. Leaders can manage attention through fear, or by using approaches rooted in what is possible. People, all people, carry some fear and doubt within, rooted in past experiences or training. The leader who sees this and fosters an environment in which people can face their fears in positive ways will achieve profound results. Instead of manipulating fear by conducting a "walk of shame," why not create a "walk of pride"? Most would want to be a part of that! The best leaders seldom judge others. They know that they cannot see the entire picture. Rather, judgment is replaced with curiosity and care.

Motivation is both rational and emotional. Why do people deal with the rational first, and then with the emotional? People are both, forever moving between these states. Many leaders tend to value the rational, leaving emotions unresolved, but feelings are one of the *gifts* human beings bring to their work, causing them to be more aware and tuned in. Research suggests that, in fact, most decisions are made emotionally, not rationally. Rational leaders who obsess over problems then become obsessed with finding causes and solutions, moving quickly to even more problems—and there is a never-ending supply! Rational process without heart is not only misguided, it is corrosive, breeds blame, and undermines learning and the human spirit at the center of motivation. If people are expected to achieve rational results imposed by others, employing rational methods and process designed by others, then they have been put into a rational prison not of their making, and with others in charge of their work. Any expectation of personal accountability in this circumstance is inauthentic, and possibly cruel. Perhaps, instead of merely solving problems rationally, leaders should first focus on achieving success and significance for the people doing the work, feeding the inevitable emotional and spiritual appetite for more.

Standardizing work comes with great risk! While simplifying things and improving both efficiency and quality, standardization can also create boredom, diminish alertness, produce more mistakes, and dampen innovation and creativity. The same old processes produce the same old results, with daily work becoming no more than a routine, a cliché, with a serious effect on individual and group engagement.

Rewards are not effective motivators. If you think rewards motivate… think again. Many reward systems punish the people for whom they are intended. Study after study demonstrate how reward systems systematically manipulate people from childhood into adulthood, undermine morale, and fail in the long term to accomplish their purposes. Using grades, money, or other extrinsic reward incentives to achieve measurable performance results often breeds a "control mindset," which depletes intrinsic motivation, the desire to do something because it is worth doing. Giving rewards implies we can withhold them (Kohn, 1993, pp. 53). "The stick is contained in the carrot… what we are talking about is the experience of being controlled and feeling punished." When we try to control people through manipulation or fear, we find that people will often distort their performance results by counter-manipulation of the data, lying, or even cheating. This is far from engagement, and is not good.

It is arrogance to think we can or should try to compel or manipulate another adult to do something they do not want to do, or even to "motivate" them to do that. Manipulation destroys relationships and engagement. Thinking that by sheer force of will you can steer the energy of others toward your dreams is an addiction, leading to the belief that if they do not do what is expected, *they* have somehow failed. Again, blaming others when things

> *"It is arrogance to think we can or should try to compel or manipulate another adult to do something they do not want to do, or even to "motivate" them to do that."*

don't work out as planned is a voluntary act of self-imprisonment. We are declaring in our blame that we have no power. Adults make choices, and master leaders respect people, offer alternatives, and guide and respect their choices. This really is not new information. When you "care" about people and attempt to "motivate" them, you had better take a hard look inside. Is it really care… or is it motivation? Or is it a disguised manipulation or demand? "I'll take care of you, but you had better take care of me!" When people fail to align with the leader's vision, motivation does not include making another somehow wrong, and then fixing them. Very few enter a relationship intending to be fixed by the other.

Engagement, emotional in nature, doesn't follow logical pathways and requires attention along the way. It is not something that can be manipulated or mandated, but emerges over time with leaders who are as loyal to staff as they expect staff to be toward them. Extraordinary leaders anchor loyalty to promises: "I will help you grow and achieve great things; I will work to keep you challenged and safe, and we can always share our experiences and learn from one another." Fostering engagement requires a mix of freedom of choice and work that is meaningful to the person doing it.

Cultivating an engaged workforce

The conditions for a motivated, engaged workforce have been known for decades, and are fairly simple. At the most fundamental level, operant conditioning confirms that, like all living creatures, people seek pleasure and avoid pain. They move toward the things they want, like, and need, and repeat behaviors that bring pleasure. People move away from things that make them uncomfortable, create frustration, and that they dislike. Further, human beings take pleasure in being part of something great, and will even endure discomfort to get it! It is alignment around shared purpose that will bring vitality to the professionals working together. Most really don't want to be told what to do, but want to know their options and be able to make choices. This is not difficult to understand, yet many leaders miss the point, thinking that they must exercise authority, cajole, preach, and use discipline to get people to do unpleasant tasks, and organize their lives around events, priorities and standardized processes not of their making. And they must do so with good cheer and high levels of energy. It is self-absorption to expect others to change merely because we want them to. Dr. Pierson's sarcasm is not an effective approach to motivate others toward great things! He may get compliance for a while, but never engagement!

Try this question: "How do we create and organize a workplace where people *freely* take personal responsibility *because they want to*?" When leadership cultivates freedom in the work, to assess, exercise judgment, decide and act, people can function professionally, fully aligned and personally accountable. Requirements to cultivate this kind of environment include:

> » *Own the responsibility* for creating an engaging environment where people can make free professional choices.

> » *Provide clarity of purpose, roles, responsibilities, needs, and consequences.* Provide knowledge about the work, performance expectations, skills, and technologies to get the work done.

> » *When decisions are needed, decide!* Own the room! Indecision is a source of anxiety, even paralysis for some. Ask a simple question: Am I deciding out of fear or possibility? Act always for possibility. Decide.

> » *Create standard work carefully.* Ensure that standard work is based on rigor, but also emphasizes the responsibility to act freely within the standards of professional practice as individuals. Never ever allow standard work to diminish to thoughtless processes and rules! Professionals, in particular, require room for the exercise of judgment.

"How do we create and organize a workplace where people freely take personal responsibility because they want to?"

» *Ensure that people have skill, competence, and confidence* to get things done (training, practice, stretch assignments). Provide necessary tools and training to use them.

» *Pay attention to people's energy and emotion.* Provide time and support for people to master the knowledge, skills, and tools to get the job done. Practice takes time and builds confidence. Pay attention to risk and reward while safeguarding the self-esteem and entrepreneurial spirit people bring to work naturally.

» *Show pride in people.* People need a measure of autonomy, a chance to practice what they know independently, to gain confidence, and to make a difference. They also need a sense that they are working as part of a community of professionals, contributing together. There is a difference between a community and a group of professionals working side by side, but not necessarily together. In a community, people can speak their mind and still be welcomed. In a group of professionals, people often feel that they must conform to group norms, a form of suppression. But when you suppress the purposeful energy of others, you generate frustration, resentment, cynicism, and even anger. All of this interferes with everything good. Learning under a microscope is seldom positive for the learner. And when people are told that in order to be valued they must be something other than who they are, the cost is huge! People, at a profound level, want to be proud of what they personally do, and the organization they work for. In a recent survey in a client organization, one staffer wrote: "I am proud to work for my company, but I am wondering if my company is proud of me." How can any leader expect employees to exhibit pride in their work if they do not feel that their leadership is proud of them? Motivation is emotional. It is the leader's job to cultivate positive emotional health among the staff.

Helping others make their personal transformations— getting to breakthrough

Extraordinary leaders help people change themselves by coaching what is needed, and why it is important. But some have the erroneous expectation that employees should think "like owners." They generally aren't owners and they won't think that way. There are people in every work environment who, for whatever reason, struggle with understanding the work or with getting themselves engaged. It is the leader's job to coach the employee through a "breakthrough" process. This is not about a simple "Aha!" moment, where an employee suddenly understands something they hadn't before. Rather, this is about a wholesale change in attitude and approach, without which the employee will fail. Master leaders do very specific things to help people "breakthrough," discussed earlier in Chapter 5:

> *"Some have the erroneous expectation that employees should think "like owners." They generally aren't owners and they won't think that way."*

» *They help the person define who they are, and what they intend. They identify their opportunities, gifts, and competency gaps.* Conversation about this requires being firm and direct about their gifts and their gaps. Such candor requires kindness, courage, and resolve for the leader, but must occur if authentic change is to take place.

» *They change the environment and expectations to support new behaviors and intentions and redefine what is possible. Then they disturb the peace!* New, clearly articulated expectations must be set. This is uncomfortable and unsettling. But it is a necessary part of the process.

» *They discover new strength by stretching and expanding the expectations.* Experimentation tests new limits, changes thinking patterns, and helps create new habits and approaches to the work.

» *They pick concrete goals, designed to exceed expectations, and act.* Momentum counts as you help others change. Without action, there will be no change and therefore no new results. Focus on what matters most for those you coach.

» *They help people change what they believe about themselves, and map out a new future.* Extraordinary leaders know that this is an "inside job," and no one can do it for another. Each of us, on our own, must define what makes a truly satisfying life and career. Without such support, anything done to create new approaches will be temporary at best, eroding as you reenter your familiar environments and daily actions. When people are being drawn by their own intentions, wants and dreams, they do not need to be motivated by anyone else.

» *They help the person create, own, and use new habits.* This is the "lock-in" phase, where behavior repetition fosters habits, and then habits become how things are done every day without a lot of conscious thought or deliberation.

Breakthrough is most intense when driven from within. Obviously, it would be best to help people make their own breakthrough, but that is not always an option. It is sometimes necessary for the leader to firmly require significant change on the part of the individual, posing the risk of job jeopardy if that change does not occur. (There will be more on this in the next chapter!) In the end, there is no such thing as disinteresting work or activity! Literally everything can bring value, learning, and energy. There are only disinterested people. The best leaders inspire people to live extraordinary lives of possibility and achievement, and remove those who cannot or will not engage.

There is no magic motivational pill

With his sarcasm, Dr. Pierson destroyed relationships, and everything suffered as a result. All broken relationships are the result of broken agreements. Blame and shame do not add value. In fact, they deplete energy and create resentment. No one moves forward. Building a rewarding, productive environment, where people are engaged in the work while satisfying themselves in the process, is not easy or simple. Bridges teaches (Bridges, 1980, p.37) that "There is, in fact, no right way, for every way has its price and its rewards." The goal is to build a self-directed, self-correcting, and self-improving community of extraordinary professionals, who get the work done with minimal supervision, and with a great deal of freedom in the use of professional judgment regarding the resources at their disposal. This requires leader awareness and skill to navigate respectful relationships, provide information, authority, and resources; and the will to insist on measurably high performance in a positive setting over time. As we move on, our legacy does not reside in the organizations we leave behind or in their products. Rather, it resides in the minds and hearts of the people we have touched with respect, care, and inspiration.

"The best leaders inspire people to live extraordinary lives of possibility and achievement, and remove those who cannot or will not engage."

Two steps on the path to cultivating respect for others

Extraordinary leaders cultivate engagement through positive relationships that are respectful, and that begin with the wants, needs, and intentions of the people doing the work. As you reflect on the messages in this chapter, consider how this applies to your leadership by answering the questions in Step 1 and taking the challenges in Step 2. Take time to reflect, listen internally to what matters most to you, and journal your what you are learning as you do this.

Step 1:

» List three things you like about the people with whom you are working.

» Do you know what they want and need from their work—not just rationally, but emotionally?

» What two things are you doing to cultivate a climate of engagement, self-confidence, trust, and high performance? How are you helping them achieve their wants and needs?

» What specific actions have you taken to make sure that every person you engage with feels appreciated and valued?

Step 2:

» Ask three staff what they want and need from their work, and publicly commit to help them achieve those wants and needs.

» Find at least one example of environmental elements impeding the work of staff. Change the environment.

» Find three opportunities this week to recognize and respect those in your charge, and do so publicly.

CHAPTER 8

Respecting Power:
Am I Willing to Pay the Price?

"Avoid relationships with people who can see good only in their position.
Anyone who vilifies the other side is creating enemies,
which is ultimately more destructive than anything else."
(Chopra, p. 174)

KEY POINTS SUMMARY

» Authentic "power" is realized in the decisions we make and the change we create.

» Never take on others' responsibilities.

» Authentic power will always face resistance.

» There is no room for bullies or blame!

» Make it clear what you will and will not do, and then stick with it (make sure what you spend your time on is important to you).

To be an extraordinary leader, you don't have to change your job or job title. You just have to change how you do that job. And this is not about "heroic" efforts, going constantly above and beyond "the call of duty." Such obsessive "heroism" leads usually to limited results. Authentic power means leading from "within," and cannot be bestowed. Rather, it is earned, one decision at a time. This means "doing the right thing," a sometimes very difficult prospect. Doing the right thing tempts resistance from others, and maybe even from within yourself. Not every decision is easy, and when the human spirit is involved, things get very complicated, many decisions coming with a price. Whenever we move forward on anything, there is likely to be some discomfort. This keeps us awake to possibility.

Consider Don's story. Don was a well-liked storeroom employee who worked long hours and was willing to do anything he was asked. Unfortunately, he injured his back moving supplies that exceeded the lifting limits of the department. His failure to wear a required lift brace resulted in tens of thousands of dollars in worker's compensation, medical, and lost-time costs, not to mention considerable pain and suffering on his part. As he mended, Don returned to work with strict lifting limits. But despite his manager's cautions, he violated those limits again and reinjured his back, which resulted in additional significant costs. Once more, Don took time to heal, and returned to work. This time, his supervisor visibly posted Don's lifting limits, instructing him to stay within them, and warned that his job would be in jeopardy if he did not. That very week, while helping someone move a large item, Don again exceeded his limits. For the third time he injured his back, and his manager wanted to terminate his employment for failure to follow instructions. The manager considered the decision to be an easy one. But there is a difference between simple and easy. Most challenges that we face today are fairly simple… but most are not easy, especially when it comes to human beings we care about. That is why they are called challenges.

Clearly, Don had no intent of complying with any limits, despite his injuries. This wasn't malicious. He wanted to be an effective team member, and didn't feel that his restrictions allowed that. Unfortunately, there was no other work Don was qualified to do within the organization, and he had no interest in training. In circumstances like this, leaders must sometimes release common wisdom about "what should be done" ("Let's give him another chance?") in favor of "what is," and then build on that. A decision was necessary, for both Don's protection and the welfare of the organization, to remove him from his position. He simply could not be trusted to take care of himself, and his risk to the organization was simply too expensive, no matter how well he performed when healthy. This is the appropriate use of authentic power, doing the right thing regardless of difficult and personal feelings.

Power is realized in making decisions

Reality doesn't care who changes things. If you do not accept the challenge, someone else will. But when change is necessary, reality will somehow make it happen. Decisions to change things are at the heart of most leadership activity, and are the basic exercise of leadership power. All of our data gathering, problem-solving, communicating, and prioritizing eventually reduce to decisions between alternative paths, and decisions about resource allocation. Often, these decisions must be made rapidly in an environment that is chaotic, with little clarity about what the "right" decision might be. Some decisions, like releasing Don, must be made with compassion, but rationally, even though they tear at the heart of any leader with a soul. This is one price that leaders pay in accepting the role.

Of course, many decisions are simply straightforward. Another story: while preparing to greet new employees for an employee orientation session, I noticed that one participant was acting a bit "strangely," his behavior suspiciously a bit "off," so I asked him to report to the health

"Reality doesn't care who changes things. If you do not accept the challenge, someone else will. But when change is necessary, reality will somehow make it happen."

nurse for a drug screen. Lab results confirmed the presence of cocaine in his system, and I immediately terminated him, contacting his hiring manager. You simply do not show up for work under the influence of an illicit drug, on your first day or any other! Of course, the hiring manager was upset, but understood the decision.

It is in decisions that leadership power is tested and skills improved over time. Friedman makes this clear (Friedman, p. 69): "When one makes a decision, one is making choices, which includes the choice of being willing to give something up." As a leader, you must pick your issues carefully, let the small things slide, and focus always on what matters most. Take a stand when necessary, but only on those things that count. Leadership courage is not about bravery, though bravery is sometimes required. Courage means to act on intention regardless of distraction, and regardless of how you feel! This is about exercising authentic competence, so that bravery is seldom needed. Such competence comes with experience in making choices that stretch our willingness to take some risk. In each of the above situations, the decision required giving something up, perhaps risking a relationship, a new employee, or even the goodwill of the manager involved. But failure to decide results in needless expense, employee morale issues, and, in some cases, injury or risk to either the employees or the people they serve. This is the extraordinary leader's challenge—making decisions requires the courage to decide with imperfect data, the willingness to face your own emotions, and the fortitude to accept criticism that your decisions might evoke. Leaders come together to plan, solve problems, and encourage one another. But in the end, they practice leadership alone. As a colleague once exclaimed, "Some decisions suck, but regret and remorse suck more!"

Is your power "authentic"?

Amateur leaders often believe that they are exercising authentic power, when in fact, they are exercising *external* power, derived from outside oneself due to position, title or some other bestowed authority. They believe that they can get more simply by asking for it, even demanding it, without any further investment on their part. Look: investing nothing seldom gets you much! Reliance on external power to demand results breeds fear, because it is born of fear: fear of failing, of looking bad, of not appearing "in charge," etc. Those who claim leadership by demanding and controlling others are at the very least abusive and perhaps, cruel. This is not mastered leadership, but rather amateurs "out of balance." Power anchored in fear rather than intention saps energy and emotional health, and leaves people feeling disempowered and victimized. When we ignore the human connections that are needed to be successful, we pay a serious price: anxiety, obsession with superficial results, and addictions to things that do not really matter. Frankly, there's nothing normal about any leader who delights in creating anxiety and discomfort in others. The result of such sick behavior will be cynicism, chaos, and ultimately failure for both leader and organization.

"Change has a twin brother named Resistance, and both brothers believe they are right in their positions."

Authentic power comes from within, and will face resistance

Authentic power is different, coming from within and from relationships. Rather than breeding fear, it encourages connectivity. Authentic leaders create energy through strength and trust in others. They know that to get things done, somebody must *do* something, usually something different, which means change. Making choices and changing things is the ultimate display of creativity, the core of the leader's power.

But Change has a twin brother named Resistance, and both brothers believe they are right in their positions. There will always be some who do not wish to make necessary changes, regardless of the leaders' decisions. In fact, you can expect that some, even some with the most to gain, will actually sabotage any steps to change things or create a new balance. Arguments occur! As Moore tells us (Moore, 2014, p. 271), "Too often, our arguments are about who is right, and who is telling the truth. We should abandon the idea of truth altogether. It only causes trouble!" Given that, some disagreement is normal, predictable, and actually a healthy thing. Peter Drucker insists (Drucker, 2002, p. 148) that "One should not make big decisions unless there has been disagreement."

Resistance is one way that people learn, test, and discover boundaries. When people resist your best efforts, it is a learning moment. You learn things you, and they, might otherwise never know. When in disagreement or conflict with someone, the most important question we can ask, though it pains us to do so, is: "Am I wrong about this?" Perhaps the resistance is a safety issue, or maybe an issue of ethics or moral behaviors. Leader impatience here is an enemy, the desire to have our needs met first. If we impatiently attempt to control people and outcomes to our preferred approaches or solutions, we prevent our own success as leaders. We must first listen, learn, and, perhaps, go and see for ourselves what is going on.

Not wanting to align has many forms

To the extent that our decisions and actions limit or disempower others, we will be met with resistance. But if the decisions have been well vetted, and people have had the opportunity to voice their ideas and concerns, then it is time to move forward. Yet some will still resist. Leaders must be aware of the many nonproductive versions of resistance, the many ways to avoid aligning with the directions that have been set by leaders. The patterns are fairly clear: griping, gossip, ally-building, rumors, catastrophizing and secrecy. Some patterns are so embedded that a manager/leader could reasonably ask, "Why do I put up with this?" Extreme resistance is disruptive, an "energy vampire," and nonproductive. Sometimes, one person can ruin the energy for everyone! Refuse to spend much time with pessimists or negative people. They will just pull you down. Some of the common resistance variations, along with possible responses/antidotes, include:

» **Dire David**: "If you make this change, the customer will suffer, and so will employees, and work won't get done!" (Really! Did the customer tell you that? I heard something different. Let's go ask.)

» **Social Sarah**: "Why don't a few of us just go have coffee and talk about this?" (Sorry, but after all we have already talked about, there is nothing further to discuss.)

» **Vicky Victim**: "We trust you, and need you to advocate for us. Don't let these changes happen." (The subtext is, if I make this change, I am part of the problem. I'm not the problem, and if you trust me, you will follow).

» **Persecuted Paula:** "Why won't you stop hurting us? No one else is going this way and making these changes." (Sorry, but I don't act just because everyone else is.)

» **Accusing Al**: "You just don't care about us, and what we need!" (I do care, but I also care about many other things, and I must prioritize.)

» **Tenacious Terri** (asked repeatedly, despite refusal)**:** "Couldn't we keep things as they are, instead of making us change? Let's fix this!" (Your persistence is admirable, but it's still no. Don't ask again, please.)

» **Sadie Suck-up:** "We admire your leadership, and I know we can count on you to keep things the way they are!" (Thanks, but it is time to get this done, and move to our next level of performance.)

» **Gang-up Gary**: "We've all talked, and we are convinced that this change is wrong-headed." (Thanks for the input, but the decision was well vetted, and the gang is wrong. Provide substantive reasons for reconsideration, or go back to work.)

» **Polly Policy:** "If you make this change, it will violate policy, certification requirements, the law, etc." (Really? Show me exactly where it says that.)

» **Joker Jack:** "What's wrong? You forget to have your coffee this morning?" (Nope. Have had two cups so far!)

Most griping like this is passive/aggressive, and reveals a victim mentality. They are not offering solutions, just delay and obstruction. By definition, they do not really know what should be done. "Those who are lost should never insist that they know the way!" (Kieves, p. 140.) What such victims fail to understand is that they have created pre-conditions for their own happiness and have put their happiness in the control of others. Truly happy people bring their happiness with them. Self-appointed victimization is negative energy that only leads to negative results. When people point at others to solve their problems for them, they are doing two things wrong: preparing the way for blame; and relinquishing their own power. Bitching and complaining solve nothing, alienate others, and drain away time and energy. Why would anyone ever go there? Some people simply love drama in their lives, as a form of adventure. They complain, and raise their own and everyone else's stress, sometimes due to boredom, and the antidote is work that has purpose. These victim scenarios are played out by people who believe that they are entitled to something they do not have. If your goal is to please others at the expense of the organization's goals, these folks will continue to ask you to do so, regardless of your needs. When you work for their approval, you are placing the power of your success in the hands of others while taking all of the blame for failures.

Self-appointed victims seek power, but not usually in the productive sense of power. Rather, they seek *vindictive* power, even tyranny. They have created "victim stories," with themselves the starring actors, and believe the stories they are telling. Such stories shape perceptions and behaviors, but everybody, including self-appointed victims, is responsible for how they process events in their lives. Those who choose to be victims are victimizing themselves, and have the power to revoke that label at any time by taking responsibility. People who live their lives as if they have no power or control over how things work out have relinquished their lives to others who will control them. They are taking no responsibility for who they are. Friedman (1999, p. 93) describes them as participants in a "chronically anxious relationship." They are convinced that the leader's decisions are somehow causing them harm, and they are expecting you to rescue them. Friedman describes their view of the world in on/off and black/white terms. They tend to be unforgiving, relentless, and have little insight into their own contribution to their focus of concern. They are easily hurt. They collect grievances and often compete for "most victimized" status, while never seeing how their victimization contributes to the problems.

So, how should the leader treat these characters? Never let people hold you hostage to their self-serving demands. It only leads to poor choices, and more hostage-taking in the future. You cannot heal fear and self-appointed victimization by using external power and demanding change. It will just make things worse, an amateur move. Those who criticize without substantive solutions and a willingness to help do not have the organization's best interests in mind. Such dissatisfaction means that some form of change is probably required. It may even lead to a new purpose for some. You cannot "transform" anybody, but you can offer choices and space for personal transformation to occur. The antidote for fear is care! But be careful here… your worst possible response is empathy. Empathy is not caring, and comes with significant issues: increased stress for everyone, and risk of things spiraling into hopelessness, manipulation, and favoritism among others ("Scientific Mind": March/April, 2017, p. 9).

Never adapt to the weakness of those around you! Courageous leaders know that it is not fear that can hurt them, but rather the decision to allow fear to determine their lives and decisions. The best decisions never come

"If your goal is to please others at the expense of the organization's goals, these folks will continue to ask you to do so, regardless of your needs. When you work for their approval, you are placing the power of your success in the hands of others while taking all of the blame for failures."

from agitation or stress. They come from heartfelt thought. There is never a good excuse for cynicism… there is always an alternative. No one has power over you unless you give them that power. It is not your job as leader to make others happy, or to satisfy their wants and needs. If people believe that the organization is supposed to make them happy, they will be very disappointed. No organization can. *That is their job*, and they, like you, must make choices. Leaders who are weak in confidence, ill-informed, or uncertain about their intentions are easy prey for the resistance peddlers in the workplace. The extraordinary leader chooses: enslavement to an emotional state that is ineffective or the exercise of courage to be an inspiring leader. Effective leaders never allow the excuses of others to determine their behaviors. As Tamara Kieves tells us: "Never take advice from unhappy people" (Kieves, p. 97). If we are not moving our intentions forward, who is? Once you are a leader, there is no one else. It is up to you!

The long-term solution is much the same for all, and summarized by Schaef: "If I want to participate in creating the future, I must be willing to give up my attachment to being a victim, and take responsibility for being an adult of my species" (Schaef, August 5). Leaders must respectfully encourage people to adapt to the organization, and not expect the organization to adapt to them. You don't get to act "entitled" until you've first taken responsibility and done something with it. People who love what they are doing seldom experience fear or anxiety while doing it.

Helping people give up their victimization requires four steps: *First*, listen to what is being said, and consider the merits before judging. There may be some truth to the concerns being raised. *Second*, spell out what is required and the consequences if people do not perform as expected. *Third*, ask for and expect support and cooperation. *Fourth*, move forward, and if things do not improve, invoke respectfully, clearly, and with confidence, the consequences spelled out earlier.

For all disruptive, resistant approaches, the ultimate antidote is a leader who is confident in the decisions being made. Let's face it: some people are just plain toxic. If you can, avoid them! If you can't avoid them, choose to spend as little time as possible with them. If they are on your staff, insist that they change, or remove them. Such people suck the energy and time from everyone around and are insensitive to their emotional responses. Extraordinary leaders are never passive in the face of those who paint themselves as victims. They challenge them to accept responsibility and ensure that the decisions are carried out and changes occur. They know that an organization's success relies on its ability—and its members'—to adapt willingly and rapidly to a changing environment, and foster self-reliance and personal accountability as the heart of lasting personal power.

There does come a point when resistance is more than just a learning process, and devolves to absolute refusal to do what is required. At a profound level, such intense resistance is weakness, combined with fear, pretending to be virtue and strength, and at the core, self-serving, empty, and dishonest. This is insubordination, a leadership test. Never hand over your right to lead to someone who wants to control you! Leaders must understand that change is not the leader's journey... it is the organization's journey. Once a decision is made, leaders must tell the truth, not what others want to hear, and move forward with certainty and quiet determination to make things happen, with or without the alignment of those who wish to continue their resistance. Those who are not clear about who they are, what they want, and what they intend will often consider such determination to be arrogant and opinionated. People have three choices: embrace the change, accept the change and live with it, or leave. This is neither fun nor friendly. However, you can respect the wishes of those who do not wish to proceed, and relieve them of their responsibilities in respectful ways, if need be.

"Leaders must respectfully encourage people to adapt to the organization, and not expect the organization to adapt to them. You don't get to act "entitled" until you've first taken responsibility and done something with it."

Holding someone accountable is code for blame!

It is not uncommon to hear some in leadership positions enthusiastically describe the need to "hold people accountable." This is a clear mark of an amateur leader who wants to blame others for things' not going well. True accountability is *self*-imposed, something that you owe others, when you make a promise. It arises from how much care you have for others, and emerges in the promises made and kept. If you must "hold someone accountable," it likely means that they have failed to keep a promise, and have therefore let you down. That is a performance issue, perhaps exposing the need for discipline.

The formula for this is simple: Responsibility and authority should be in a 1:1 relationship. To make someone responsible for something and not give them the authority to act on that responsibility is unfair, and even cruel. Likewise, accountability for the promises you make can only occur to the extent that you have both the responsibility and authority to act. Without both, you cannot be accountable, expected to keep your promises. This set of ratios must be kept in balance, or the default position is blame. When digging deeper into performance problems of individuals or departments, it is common to find ratios out of balance. People are being asked to do things without the required resources, authorities, etc. Recognize that no one gets up on Monday morning eager to go to work so that the boss "can hold them accountable."

There is no place for bullies!

When amateur leaders use anxiety to motivate, it is never about the work; it's about relationships and control. Yet, it's simply foolish to try to control everyone and everything. In fact, any effort to control is the first act toward destroying any sense of community. Tom, an engineering manager, is a case in point. He was fidgeting nervously in his chair when I entered his office for our scheduled meeting about a recent employee opinion survey. His data was very positive, and at first glance, departmental staff were highly engaged, loved their work, and thought very highly of Tom. However, on closer inspection, literally every one of the forty-five surveys from his department was completed in the precise same way, every item checked the same, and none included written comments. Something was not right. When I pointed out the results and my concerns about the data, Tom became angry! "I told them to never make me look bad again after the last survey, and now look at what they've done! Somebody will pay for this!"

So, let's examine how this worked for Tom. His staff answered the previous survey honestly. As a result, he "blamed and shamed" them, and bullied them about the feedback and warned them to make him look good in the future, or else. They then organized themselves in a protective manner, did exactly what he told them to do, with the result of the next survey being exactly what he demanded from them, with the predictable opposite result of what he intended. Blaming and shaming are bullying, and he bullied them. They responded. When I met with Tom's staff confidentially, they told me that they had hoped I would see the pattern! What they did was deliberate. They bullied him back in this passive/aggressive response, and now he wanted to bully them again, making them "pay." This escalation is again predictable, and amateurish. Tom's tone changed when told that I was prepared to recommend his immediate termination if he did anything of the kind. Such retaliation would not be courageous, as his bravado suggested. What takes courage is to find a better, more productive way to relate to his staff. Staff knew that no one has that power over them unless they grant that power. They did not settle for living in fear.

There is a difference between being strong and being a bully. Bullies tend to be closed, controlling, win/lose in conflict, grandiose in their self-perceptions, and seldom admit failure. A strong leader, on the other hand, will

"Recognize that no one gets up on Monday morning eager to go to work so that the boss "can hold them accountable.""

121

approach people openly, and will engage with honesty and a win/win mindset, with realistic expectations of others. To the strong leader, failure is learning. Blame is a form of bullying. People blame one another because it is easier than taking personal responsibility for the facts and conditions of their own lives. Blame is a destructive form of false power, a total abdication of authentic power. Employing "blame and shame" approaches to motivate people generates negative reactions, taking many forms: withdrawal, avoidance, anger, malicious compliance, sabotage, cynicism, and eventually, outright rebellion. Such power struggles prevent the intimacy required to create community. Competition for power/control lies at the heart of all corporate quarrels. In such struggles, winning never heals, because it is not anchored in what matters most… personal meaning and connection. A history of this behavior results in a cultural framework of deep-seated caution, anxiety, gossip, back-biting, and antagonism. "Bullying" behavior is intimidation, and tolerating any measure of it leads to depression, and a completely disempowered staff. Just one person can contaminate the energy of everyone else around, polluting the entire environment. Bullying leaders who cannot overcome the temptations of power, greed, and grandiosity are giving themselves permission to be irresponsible leaders.

Extraordinary leaders cultivate a positive, authentic form of power to get things done

Authentic power thrives in an environment of mutual respect and care. People need to act freely within their professional disciplines, and be able to master their professional skills. When you create the conditions for people to act freely without fear, you also create the conditions for personal accountability, where people can make choices and promises. Without such freedom, there can be no accountability. Most come to the workplace with good intentions, wanting to contribute and make a difference, but they require an orderly environment to feel balanced. They have not chosen to work in an environment of fear and intimidation, or to be controlled. Such a choice would be a decision to be miserable.

To bring about more balance, the extraordinary leader attends to four very important factors in building a respectful, productive culture.

1. *Develop people's vision and competencies.* Extraordinary leaders inevitably have visions that are much bigger than themselves or their immediate tasks. People need to understand the vision, and have the time in practice to become great at what they are doing. Leaders know that, and provide room for personal growth and learning.

2. *Create a team expectation.* Little is done in isolation today, and people must learn the skills required to be interdependent. Again, this takes experience over time, and must be reinforced by leader expectations.

3. *Cultivate personal accountability through input in standardized process design.* People are not machines. They require dialogue for understanding what is required, and co-authorship to effect buy-in. The extraordinary leader understands the value that comes with engaging people in the design of the work that they are doing, and waste little precious time waiting for the approval or support of others.

4. *Develop personal accountability through self-chosen metrics.* Again, this requires dialogue for better understanding. Extraordinary leaders encourage such dialogue, and come to the conversation willing to have their opinions influenced. They not only listen, but take seriously the advice and opinions of those doing the work. We are most effective in helping others change when we are openly and visibly willing to be changed ourselves, and not let our own opinions get in the way. Only then can we be true colleagues, learning and growing together.

"We are most effective in helping others change when we are openly and visibly willing to be changed ourselves, and not let our own opinions get in the way."

These four steps will be treated in more detail in the next chapter, which will focus on the challenges and obstacles inherent in professional leadership practice.

Fundamentals of leading others—a new contract:

Improving performance requires focus. We must first determine what matters most, and second, remove all distractions. Then we must act, and apply resources to the critical few. Authentic power is not the ability to exert your will over others. Such power is temporary at best, deflating, and reveals a core of fear and anxiety rather than confidence and peace. When we act to disempower others, we choose to abstain from offering respect. Authentic power is rooted in positive, caring intention, combined with focused energy. Acting as a leader means writing a clear and unequivocal "new contract" with yourself and others. Be certain that the intentions in that contract are *your* intentions. If not, you will fail to live up to the terms of your own contract and will fail as a leader. You are not limited to the four points below, but they're a good start:

1. Be absolutely clear about intentions, with conviction and certainty. Are we focused on what is expected of us or on those things that would lead to something great?

2. Be absolutely passionate in work, caring for those who are helping achieve the intentions. They deserve your energy and care.

3. Take nothing for granted, and avoid personal attachment to your own methods. Be open to the ideas of others, and inevitable changes in context and plan. At the same time, never let the criticism of others bring you down. To do so requires your participation.

4. Always put your energy into your work in a way that engages you emotionally, and is visible to those around you, so that they know you care.

A contract like this is simple to articulate, but very difficult to execute consistently. Mark Nepo warns that the fact that "we will fail and fall, and make mistakes, is not newsworthy. It is in facing what we've done or failed to do and how we got up that our character is defined" (Nepo, 2007, p.177). Rising to the challenges such a contract brings has many benefits: to the leaders, confidence, certitude, character, focus, personal power; to the followers, clarity, understanding, alignment. To the extent that you live such a contract and align with the intentions of the organization, the price of leadership is worth paying. Will you rise to the challenge, and pay the price?

Two steps on the path to cultivating respect for power

Extraordinary leaders must respect authentic power as a very real presence in their work. They must also understand resistance to that power, and how to address that resistance when it occurs. As you reflect on the messages in this chapter, consider how this applies to your leadership by answering the questions in Step 1 and taking the challenges in Step 2. Take time to reflect, listen internally to what matters most to you, and journal what you're learning.

Step 1:

> » Identify three things you can do to create a sense of possibility and goodwill. What will cause people to want to contribute?

> » What three things can you do to respond effectively to the negative energies that some bring to the work?

> » Name three "victims" in the workplace and determine how you will address them.

Step 2:

» Define three ways to exercise power by doing the right thing to enable your staff to be successful in some way that they are not today. Do it!

» Meet with three "self-appointed victims," one at a time, to point out their responsibilities for bringing about change in their situations. Offer to help them, to the extent that they take responsibility for helping themselves.

» Ask for support from each individual, and assure them that you will help if they wish your help. If the victim behavior continues, invoke the appropriate consequences.

» Write your "new contract" and share with each individual.

CHAPTER 9

Respecting Challenges and Obstacles

*"A leader needs the capacity not only to accept the solitariness
that comes with the territory, but also to come to love it."*
—*Friedman, p.19*

KEY POINTS SUMMARY

» Extraordinary leaders cultivate personal accountability.

» There are four steps to restore balance during change-
related chaos.

» Intrinsic motivation is more profound than extrinsic motivation.

» Buy-in requires co-authorship.

» People should know better… but they don't!

» Blame and shame is counter to the foundational "respect
for people."

» Intuition is a gift. Use it!

» Not everything is a problem to be solved.

» Foster independent work, not dependency. Deal with
"learned helplessness."

» Respect the legacy of those who have gone before, on whose you
are building yours.

It is not possible to know what you are capable of until you confront the real tests of leadership. Every day presents challenges, threats, and obstacles, causing many to refrain from even taking on the leader role. The extraordinary leader embraces the role, and knows that leadership requires that we make choices every day. The future is shaped by the decisions that you make today, and failure to decide leaves your future in the hands of others.

Making choices is never easy, especially those that require giving up something or someone we love to gain something or someone we love. Either way, a piece of us must die. The best leaders seldom give much thought to possible loss, and focus instead on intention, knowing that you get what you focus on. They know that learning means changing things, often at the expense of comfort and stability. The leader must be OK with uncertainty, difficult questions, absence of easy answers, and risk. They ignore anything pessimistic, trusting in themselves and in the wisdom of those around them. Such leaders also realize that, if they are on a path that will not allow them to achieve their intentions, they can lower their expectations or change the path they're on. The extraordinary leader will most often choose a new path, knowing that they always have more choices than those immediately present. This all begins with leaders who cultivate personal accountability for themselves, and for the people around them.

Extraordinary leaders cultivate personal accountability

As leaders change things, the resulting chaos often comes as a surprise, and throws people out of balance. Jake was a loading dock worker who served on the company profit-sharing committee. After a particularly intense meeting focused on the need for reducing waste and cutting costs, he returned to his work station and found the soda distributor waiting to unload his delivery of vending colas and other soft drinks. Jake mentioned that the company was on a cost-savings initiative, and told the distributor that the company might be looking for competitive bids from other vendors soon. The distributor immediately called his company sales office, and was authorized to make an immediate 10 percent price reduction, saving the company literally thousands of dollars annually.

Most people would see what Jake did as a good thing, and might commend him for his initiative. But in this case, the internal purchasing folks were not "most people," and they were not happy. They were upset that Jake "violated procedure," failed to conform to purchasing policy, and "acted irresponsibly" in representing the company's interest. They were angry and embarrassed, and wanted him disciplined. What started as an innocent conversation became a chaotic mess, with Jake in the middle. When people show up with such anger and resentment, it is fair to ask if they are really focused on helping, or on making a difference. Circumstances are not what make people angry… the anger is already there, and the circumstance is merely pretext for its release.

"The future is shaped by the decisions that you make today, and failure to decide leaves your future in the hands of others."

Leaders do four things to ensure balanced action

When circumstances move us into a chaotic state, it is our job as leaders to slow things down, even stop, so that we can understand. Only then is it possible to take meaningful, balanced action. Anger can be helpful, always has a reason, and if we stay with it long enough, we may learn something important. It can actually bring a form of clearing for new pathways toward intention, but it can also be divisive and damaging. The need is for balance. In the last chapter, we said that to cultivate balanced action, four things were necessary, done well before the chaos ensues:

1. ***Develop people's competencies!*** Talent development is probably the single most important work done by leaders. Do you treasure the gifts that people bring to their work and develop them further? Talent

development strengthens both individual and team performance by raising competency levels, and ultimately the confidence of everyone, along with their willingness to increase responsibility and challenge. Developing people sends a clear message that people are important, an asset and not a liability, and that their contribution is valued. It is then that people are comfortable making promises to do new things and continue their growth.

2. ***Create a team expectation:*** It is wise to remember that not everything requires teams, and further, some things really are better done by individuals. When imposed, team processes can become stiff, without flow and with many collisions, all of which affects relationships. One medical practice, in their business charter, required 100 percent "team consensus" on all decisions affecting the partners, reducing the partnership to a paralyzed state in which it was impossible to make any decision at all since the rules gave everyone veto power! This is tyranny pretending to be teamwork. But leadership is an emotional process, and teams are powerful, emotional mechanisms that can take you where individuals simply cannot go. Synergies and other benefits have been well documented. But teams require nurturing, a human process that's an emotional journey To succeed, teams also require effective decisional processes to deal with disagreement, shared responsibility and accountability, and the attention of leadership on the dynamics among team members.

3. ***Cultivate personal accountability through standard work.*** People require a certain amount of order. Change creates stress and even chaos, and if this is not addressed, people will never feel grounded or secure. Standardizing work processes and metrics adds to clarity for people, but it comes with consequences. Standardizing clarifies steps, specifies assignments, and makes waste visible. But doing so unavoidably irritates some, who feel that this replaces professional freedom of action with controlling and autocratic process, specifically threatening morale and the sense of dignity required for engagement. When we build standardized process and methods, it is important that we hold them loosely, not tightly. There is a balance: too loose,

and there is no standard, too tight, and you risk the very factors that bring purpose and meaning to the work. If properly designed and implemented, standard work actually is respectful. Bringing people together to create the standardized processes, tools, and actions creates co-authorship, and the freedom to work within the professional disciplines that they bring to the work. Such an approach increases engagement, builds confidence, and encourages improvement over time, with staff fully engaged in making sure that the improvements really are improvements for the customer and the business. Standardized process actually sets the stage for innovation, where people find new answers to old questions. Paradigm shifts require new questions.

"Leadership is an emotional process, and teams are powerful, emotional mechanisms that can take you where individuals simply cannot go."

4. ***Develop personal accountability through self-chosen metrics.*** Carefully choosing the metrics to be followed and how you go about tracking those metrics makes a difference in the attention people pay to their work. It is easy to get this wrong.

Of course, we tend to abhor those things that disturb us. This is natural! But in that disturbance, there is opportunity to grow and learn. If we avoid this, the disturbance will control us. Remember Jake and the soda price reductions? After many meetings to sort things out and take a pause, the purchasing folks and shipping dock folks decided they had to work as a team and had not been doing so. Expectations and understandings were recalibrated, and Jake was not only *not* disciplined, he was given a bonus for his initiative! This occurred because the leaders involved realized that the company's interests were most important, and that the other issues and concerns were not what mattered most. The "crisis" became an opportunity for leaders to clearly define reality, as it is. But this took conversation and a great deal of reflection. Leaders must embrace the responsibility to continually transform themselves. Failure to do so is not leadership, merely reactive impulse based on past scripting and experience that likely does not apply to now.

Intrinsic motivation is more powerful than extrinsic motivation.

Another story: A group of legal partners was working to improve how policy and procedures were organized for better efficiency. The manager had suggested several ideas that seemed to have merit, in both cost savings to the business and quality for the client. In extending them, she offered a number of customer satisfaction-related changes in metrics that would be the right thing to do and would lower costs. However, one of the partners raised his hand and rubbed his thumb and his index finger together several times in the universal sign language for "cash." "If you want me to do the right thing, then you give me some of this," he said. "I'll do the right thing if I see the money!" It hadn't occurred to the manager that the customer metrics would hold such little weight, and that the partner would need to see the immediate financial benefit to him personally. Surprised, she asked, "What about the quality of work we are doing for the client?"

So, what has happened to create this level of thinking? Kohn described this phenomenon by showing how we confuse intrinsic and extrinsic motivation. It is possible to cause someone who is motivated intrinsically (to do things because they are the right things to do) to shift over time to extrinsic motivation ("I'll only do it if you give me something in return"). Such a shift is often a tragedy, bringing about decisions and behaviors that are devoid of human spirit. Yet this shift occurs every day in most of our organizations. The use of piecework compensation processes, pay-for-performance systems, individual incentive bonuses, and other extrinsically organized rewards have the effect of repeatedly undermining the intrinsic reasons for professionally being in the work in the first place. As one survey respondent put it recently, "No one comes to work here motivated to reduce costs." Simply put, most people see cost management as leadership's job, not theirs. Ken Blanchard cautions further: "When managers focus their attention only on fiscal measurements, they have their eye on the scoreboard and not on the ball" (Ken Blanchard, "Passion Promotes Profit," CLO magazine, 9/2012). This is not a small thing. If you want true engagement and individual motivation, organize the workplace to value people's intrinsic and personal reasons for being there.

People should know better... but they often don't!

Often, our path in leadership requires dealing with distasteful, boring, or frustrating situations. It seems that the more important an initiative is to the organization, the more resistance you will feel. Actually, this is how we continue to learn and grow. There are many obstacles that interfere with leaders as they work to deal with change effectively. All focus on behaviors that could be labeled "people should know better," behaviors that seem to increase in frequency during times of turbulence and anxiety. The temptation is to deny reality, and work around them rather than learn from and deal with them directly. As leaders, we cannot save people. We can only be present to them, and help them once they are ready for that help. The list of obstacles is long, and includes, but are not limited to, those deconstructed below:

The Pretense of empowerment: Most people start their first job or a new job, ready to shine. Early passion is innocent, unknowing of the obstacles and challenges ahead. Mature passion accepts those obstacles as part of the joy of the work. They want to contribute. Unfortunately, work conditions and leader intentions sometimes dull that shine, or even obliterates it in some. Often, a leader will request

"The more important an initiative is to the organization, the more resistance you will feel. Actually, this is how we continue to learn and grow."

help, stating: "I have decided, and want people to buy in to it!" This is troubling, more so when they then ask a consultant to help create buy-in. The leader has already made the decision, and is asking for help to manipulate people by achieving this thing called buy-in, when in fact what the leader really wants is compliance. Certainly, there are genuine compliants, "good soldiers" who will accept any decision with energy, if the assignment comes from the leader. But this is not buy-in. If you want compliance, ask for it. If you want buy-in, offer co-authorship, involve the stakeholders in the decision, no pretense, no manipulation. Asking for buy-in while meaning compliance, can only create cynicism.

The blame/shame game: Perfection is not the leader's friend. Pursuit of perfection can only lead to fear of failure and paralysis. Progress occurs one imperfection at a time. People often expend much energy either blaming or shaming those around them when things don't go well. Such judgment is one of the most serious obstacles there is to leader success, whether that be self-judgment, or judgment by others of others. First, they blame specific people, then the process. When that fails, they conclude that the system must be at fault. Eventually, if pushed into a corner, they might consider that some of the fault might lie with themselves.

Blaming and shaming are contagious, and demoralizing. It is even done in advance! "If you fail to act now, you will have a disaster on your hands, and it will be your fault!" No one wants to be blamed, but most have participated in it. Such behavior reveals people unable to deal with their own emotional ups and downs, and it is unlikely that any leader participating in this will be able to deal effectively with others. Blaming is actually illogical behavior, emotionally charged and self-absorbed, and can transform any business into a co-dependent, fear-based group of people. You can't be a blaming leader without breeding distrust, creating much misunderstanding and painful situations. Fortunately, new patterns can be learned, requiring the exercise of will, and absolute insistence that blaming and shaming are poisons unacceptable in the workplace. The problem is not "those guys"! *Start* by considering your own contribution to the situation.

Data is good, intuition is bad! One of the powerful gifts of our human nature is our intuition. This is a birthright, and many today have lost touch with it. Somehow, in the press for efficiency and clarity of goals in the pursuit of improvement and excellence, metrics and data have become preeminent. There is value in this, but it can go too far. One prominent process improvement speaker (whom I will keep anonymous out of self-protection) once declared in my presence that "data equals truth!" No, it doesn't. Data is data, and without analysis, nothing more. Anecdotally, there are numerous stories of people following their GPS signal into lakes and rivers, mindlessly ignoring what is in front of them while depending on data that was inaccurate. Additionally, not everything can be measured (try measuring the love of a spouse or child or the fear or courage someone exemplifies), and often, things that can be measured are not worth measuring. Data, metrics, and targets are usually simple on the surface, but what we do with them is usually complicated. Failure to exercise thoughtful caution in their use will only accomplish unintended behaviors and consequences, likely not good.

"If you want buy-in, offer co-authorship, involve the stakeholders in the decision, no pretense, no manipulation. Asking for buy-in while meaning compliance, can only create cynicism."

Intuition, hunches, and general feelings about things must be respected, not criticized as being nothing more than a guess. Neuroscientist Antonio Damasio tells us that "Our feelings decide for us 95 percent of the time" (quoted in Robbins, p. 91). Intuition can be a source of important information, borne of experience over time, an innate wisdom that emerges from a lifetime of learning and practice. To respect your intuition is to acknowledge that not everything can be explained in rational terms. Orloff describes intuition (Orloff, p. 21) as "a truth-detector" enabling rapid understanding and conclusions. Every successful physician has followed intuitive paths for assessment, diagnosis, and treatment. Every successful investigator has followed intuitive hunches in the pursuit of truth. Every invention has been conceived in the intuitive wisdom of its inventor. No amount of rational thought can truly reflect the whole of your experience, making your intuitive gifts not only necessary but also enriching. Failure to heed intuition can lead to fatigue, energy loss, despair, a sense of being "out of touch." It is what allows you to make decisions in the absence of perfect information, which is usually the case.

Respect for intuition is of particular interest to the author, due to a personal experience over forty years ago. While making an evening "bread/milk run" for my young family (two babies in the house at the time), I drove to a nearby corner store. As I exited my car, my intuition told me to get back in, lock the door and drive on. But I dismissed it as irrational, since I had no logical reason to be afraid. I went into the store, bought my supplies, and on leaving, encountered three teenagers, one on each side, and one directly in front who held a gun pointed directly at me. He ordered me into the backseat of my own car with his two accomplices and drove us away to a secluded park, where I was beaten, stripped of my valuables, and told to run or I would be shot. Had I listened to my intuition in the first place, I might have avoided a truly dangerous situation! Somehow, a part of me knew that something was amiss, but I did not listen, and paid the consequences. Today I pay very close attention to my intuition!

Intuition does not come with standard work process and a requirement for more data. Intuition is a form of knowing, without really knowing why. No one will ever have all of the information about anything, and actually, the "answers" are not usually in the data anyway. Only an arrogant leader will try to anticipate every problem or obstacle to the plan by continuously and obsessively collecting data. It is better to act on imperfect information and learn from experience. Believing that the answers are in the data dooms you to obsession with certainty, propelling a desire for more data and causing you to spend less time on decisions and improvement. Frankly, in a competitive world, those who insist (usually with a critical edge) on mountains of data deserve to fail. It is paralyzing in a fast-changing world, where intention and the ability to decide are more important than data-gathering. Most decisions today are not yes/no, right/wrong, good/bad, black/white. Most are gray… the data will not decide for you. It is time to grow up and deal with risk and uncertainty. Leaders must have a bias for reliance on others who have more knowledge, skill, and practical wisdom, all of which usually comes with a healthy dose of intuition. It is always available, and can be developed by listening to what is going on "inside."

Let's define the problem! Often, especially in performance-improvement events and activities, when people come together to discuss things, someone states in a serious, profound tone, "Let's define the problem!" When there is a problem in front of the group, this is appropriate. We will always have problems to solve and broken things to fix. The reasons: there are always more wrong ways to do things than right, and it is always easier to break things than to keep them new. But not everything is a problem to be solved or something to be subjected to group process. When you hold this view of the world, your analytically trained mind offers little room for things like discovery, joy, serendipity, and just plain fun. Sometimes, people just need to talk, share insights and observations, encourage one another, and simply share their pain. Treating pain as a problem to be solved is futile and creates a life controlled by pain. Perhaps the pain has a purpose, and will lead to new opportunity! Why do people seem to feel that, if they just reduce things to a problem to be solved, they can "fix it"? The analytical process, misused, actually becomes a club to wield, inflicting damage rather than adding value. Not everything requires a root-cause analysis, and not everything needs a group convened to find solutions. That is not how life works!

While it is heresy to many in the process-improvement world, perhaps the best way to reduce worry and stress and improve performance is to take the focus off problems and the stories that come with them. Rather, we should focus more on intention, and stories that are inspiring and optimistic. The best leaders recognize that

"Intuition is a form of knowing, without really knowing why. No one will ever have all of the information about anything, and actually, the "answers" are not usually in the data anyway."

the symptoms of life are a form of wealth, not concern. There will always be highs and lows. When you can sense that something is not as it should be, then you have an opportunity to grow and transcend the present with an inspiring vision for the future.

Learned helplessness: There are people who never seem to know how to do what is asked of them. Their refrain, "I don't know what to do," is consistent, penetrating, and relentless. Training does not help them, and no explanation satisfies them. They still claim not to know what to do. Or they might say, "Yes, I know what to do, but give me the tool." And then, "Give me another tool." All of this is stalling, anchored in a "poverty" and dependency mindset. Time spent trying to help people who do not want help or don't take advice seriously is time wasted. People should not have a poverty mindset unless they are in poverty. Most are not. Rather they are flooded with waste all around, missing the abundance that is theirs to use. In their dependence, these "helpless souls" are hijacking the leaders' inner purpose and intentions, who then reacts to the "imperatives" of others, rather than following their own path. It is important to care for others, but be careful of *doing* for them. People need to do for themselves, and when they must, it elicits energy, creativity, imagination, and a sense of accomplishment. If people are not placed in a position of having to accomplish for themselves, they will not learn to succeed.

Frankly, nothing will occur with these folks until there is an insistence that they experiment, and maybe succeed, maybe fail, and certainly learn from their experience. They need to quit complaining about their limits and find the opportunity to shine, improvise, and grow. Much of what brings strength to people is acquired over time and through challenging experience. When we have painful experiences, we have two choices: avoid the experience or learn and grow from it so it never again creates pain. People have been given imagination to create things, and must be encouraged to make choices with imperfect information. This brings paradox, and mistakes will occur. What seems right might be wrong, and learning from experience can be costly. But you can make your life hard or easy by the attitude you choose and the intentions you focus on. There's a difference between being compassionate and kind and being indulgent with those who refuse to act in their own behalf. Being indulgent is usually demeaning. Insist that people stretch and grow.

We need a policy on that! A "Perfect Paul" manager once insisted that I write a policy stating that customer service is a priority. When asked why such a policy was required, he recounted several instances in which customers were not being served well, by people *in his own department.* It was his belief that, unless there was a policy stating that customer service was a priority, he had no authority to correct or discipline his staff for failure to serve the customer. (You can read my thoughts between the lines on this one. No such policy was executed.) The manager was informed that he had the latitude to ensure that customers were well served, and that he, as a manager, was expected to act, with or without a policy.

"Time spent trying to help people who do not want help or don't take advice seriously is time wasted."

Every day presents opportunity to pursue what matters most. Yet many spend their days dealing with the trivial. Most leaders do not have the time or resources to write and administer paralyzing policies and standard work for every possible event or concern, nor should they. If small things disturb you, then that is who you are… small. Most of what people obsess over is just that… small. Sometimes, the most effective thing you can do is nothing. Writing policy or standardizing work should never mean abdicating management decision-making to thoughtless processes! There is nothing creative or excellent about adhering to the standards and expectations of faceless others, through policy and standard work.

Naïve wisdom: Frequently, obvious nonsense passes as wisdom. A good example is the adage, "The teacher hasn't taught until the student has learned." In some quarters, this phrase seems axiomatic in the world of learning and education, and surfaces frequently as a leadership premise. This adage is a device prompting a forced accountability on those in the teaching profession when students, for whatever the reason, fail to learn. On the surface, it seems correct. But dig deeper and find interesting truths. For this adage to be correct, the teacher must have full control over every variable that affects the learning process. This includes the environment, the knowledge and resources used in teaching, the mental attitude and approach of the student, the student's environment, all the possible learning technologies required in order to understand the individual's learning needs and wants, and the skill to apply the right approaches to address those needs and wants. The simple math underlying this set of dynamics is easy to calculate: the teacher is not solely responsible for the student's learning and never will be. Yet it's being touted as a leadership principle, a learning principle, and a "profound lesson" in fostering knowledge and wisdom. Totally naïve! There are others: "Change must start at the top," "it's about the process, not the people," and "data equals truth." They're all misguided and largely wrong.

We need a team-building session. Managers frequently ask for topical training sessions, often about team-building, time management, stress reduction, conflict management, emotional intelligence, or some other popular "topic of the month." These requests seem genuine, coming from managers who have a true desire for their departments to learn necessary skills. Team-building, when appropriate, is helpful. However, we often find other things are going on as well. Oftentimes, the manager will say to me, "you go ahead and lead the session, but I won't be able to be there. The department is really struggling with this, and *they* need the skills to manage this better." This is about showcasing, not learning, and is demeaning to the staff, in that "they need to learn this, but I don't." If the leaders know the topic, they should teach it. Furthermore, if they want others to invest time and energy in this learning process, it is also worth their time. Phony learning is a waste of time, and will create no real value for people unless leaders are present and engaged with their staff.

Let me tell you what to do... Some leaders believe that their job is to tell their staff what to do, how to do it, when to do it, where to do it, and even why to do it. Ultimately, they want it done their way, for their purposes, and have no respect for the individual work styles, knowledge, or interests of the people who are actually going to do the work. Such leaders are fostering dependency on the leader rather than growing their staff to be independent, and interdependent on one another.

One of the most difficult realities of leadership is recognizing that you are not in charge of the path people are on. The more you try to control people, manage events, and drive results, the sooner you find yourself frustrated and disappointed. When people feel controlled or "boxed in," their energy drains, satisfaction declines, and resentment and frustration builds. The problem is that, as leaders, we want recognition on our own terms, based on our perceptions of our contributions and talents, but ignoring our human flaws. This is disingenuous. Eventually, this manager will voice concerns that nobody around them is functioning well. They will ask for more training and development because their staff is unskilled and they no longer have time to tell them what, when, and how to do it, while expressing extreme frustration that everyone around them is so incompetent. This is a losing game! Sustainable change requires the development of self-reliance and personal accountability.

Disparaging the past and past leaders. Why is it that new leaders seem to find it necessary to discount and criticize those who have gone before them? This behavior is incredibly disrespectful, and usually very wrong. Typically, the "current state" is a function of literally hundreds or even thousands of decisions made by others in the past, given the best information and abilities at the time. When leaders engage in disparaging their predecessors, they reveal a complete disregard for the value of an enterprise's history and culture, and also a complete naiveté regarding

"One of the most difficult realities of leadership is recognizing that you are not in charge of the path people are on."

141

how things occur over time. All leaders stand on the shoulders of giants, and need to respect and even celebrate those giants.

We always have choices!

Understand that energy never lies! All of these situations reveal a superficial, irresponsible level of maturity and misspent energy that are leading nowhere. Leaders seem more willing to deal with chronic discomfort in these situations than more intense discomfort that would solve the problem. Instead of acting, they are reacting in fear. Two things reveal that fear: a failure to decide, and the ensuing drama between people affected over time. The antidote to both is taking action to move forward. In all of these situations, leaders are abdicating their responsibilities, and failing the test of leadership. The most telling symptom is argument. For some reason, people seem to want to argue with one another. When was the last time an argument resulted in you or another changing their mind?

Never put up with people who disrespect leadership or the work of the business. Set boundaries, communicate responsibilities, and then, when boundaries are exceeded, enact the consequences. Professional leaders know that they must work with limits and boundaries. They also know that changing things means being willing to confront those things that are currently stable, in control, safe, and even comfortable. But rather than resenting the need for change, they view change as opportunity for creativity and innovation. Exercising the ability to choose a course of action means never being "stuck." We always have choices, and there is always a next step, never a guarantee. But it begins with the leader.

Many believe that insight will motivate unmotivated people to change. Lifetimes of experience say otherwise (smoking, obesity, political behaviors, etc.). People place unreasonable demands on this world. "Satisfy me, engage me, make me feel important, keep me safe, reward me, but don't expect me to take any risk!" No one can do this for people, no one. In every case above, the effective response must begin with that one-word sentence, "No!" You are not going to do things this way. Expect that you will hear from critics when you do this. It is a given, but you don't have to listen to them. If we define the messed-up reality we've created and then try to clean up the mess with the same psychology that we used to create it, we are headed to truly disastrous results. It may be time to change our approach. At times, it is the leader's job to decide, despite the will of critics. People can choose to learn or not, to grow or not, to survive or not, to surround themselves with people who have both the competency to do the work and the willingness to contribute or not. Understanding these choices leads to clarity that begins with the simple word "no." Leadership practice requires that you give yourself to a different way of thinking and working with others, one that combines rigor with intuition and allows discovery and learning in the process of planning and doing.

"We always have choices, and there is always a next step, never a guarantee."

Two steps on the path of dealing with challenges

Leaders must be prepared to deal with the many challenges and obstacles they will confront in their leadership practice. Many have been outlined in this chapter. As you reflect on the messages here, consider how they apply to your leadership by answering the questions in Step 1 and taking the challenges in Step 2. Take time to reflect, listen to what matters most to you, and journal what you're learning.

Step 1:

» What behaviors have you been guilty of in this chapter? Why?

» What three steps can you take to approach things more effectively?

» Do any of your staff behave this way? Why?

>> How might you coach them to behave more effectively?

Step 2:

>> Identify three "giants" in your leader experience (living or not) and define what you have learned from them. Contact someone in this group and discuss what you are learning about your leadership. Ask for their advice.

>> Identify how are others dependent on you. Examine how this happened, and define three steps you can take to foster more independent action on their part. Then do it.

>> Identify three people to grant twice as much authority, responsibility, and personal accountability for the work they have today. Then determine with them their readiness to take on more. Give it to them.

PART 3

Deepening the Learning—
The Practice of Leadership

Knowledge is based on fact. Culture is based on experience and opinion anchored in experience. Both are very real! Some believe that leadership is about technique, measurable steps in a process or certain management behaviors that somehow result in people behaving in specific ways to help the organization. However, technique masquerading as leadership is not leadership. We do not find our voice as leaders through technique or through imitating others who have "the right technique." Nor do we find it in obsession with measures of process. In fact, such obsession might be a major cause of failure to grow and succeed as leaders. Rather, we find our leadership voice in our own struggles, and in the answers that we experience.

Personal growth as a leader is not like learning a skill, with incremental milestones and measures along the way. It is more about integrating many diverse learnings, and a growing awareness of personal strength, with a dropping away of weakness. To the degree that we are open and willing to listen, life will always teach us. Being a leader requires shifting gears from striving to learning, and from reaching to being present. There can be no real learning unless it engages the whole human being as an integrated mind, heart, and spirit. Leaders who fail to make this shift fail to truly lead.

The chapters in Part 3 of this book are about learning and growth for the leader, and for those who follow that leader. The extraordinary leader cares about learning, seeks out opportunities to stretch and grow, and exemplifies the humility that comes with appreciating differing perspectives, something new, and opportunities to see things in new ways. Leading from mind, heart, and spirit requires such learning. So the question is: what must I learn and how? You've read this far... read on.

CHAPTER 10

The Culture Will Teach You— Go and See, Then Do!

"The public is right to distrust traditional leaders."
—Drucker, 1989, p. 108

 KEY POINTS SUMMARY

» We misunderstand the power of culture and how it changes.

» Leadership is more than what we know.

» We are not "organizations."

» The culture lives in our conversations and sustains itself in our stories.

» We overestimate our ability to change others.

» If we change ourselves and our conversations, the culture will follow. For leaders, cultural change means personal transformation.

» There are several principles that underlie cultural change.

Entering the office, I looked around at the walls. Curiously, I saw not one, not two, not even three, but *seven* pictures of John Wayne in multiple poses. Displayed prominently were prints of John Wayne on a horse, John Wayne leaning on a fence, and even John Wayne in a black velvet wall hanging. There were also several sculptures of the Old West actor/cowboy, riding a galloping horse. Not only that, Nick, the executive VP, had replaced the company founder's portrait in the front lobby with a large rendering of, you guessed it, John Wayne. My visit was a response to Nick's request for training for his manufacturing plant executives. Nick had a twenty-year reputation for audacity, but I had never met him in person. His assistant invited me to take a chair in his office, assuring me that Nick would be by soon. *Clearly*, I thought, whimsically wondering if the guy might ride in on a horse, *this guy likes John Wayne.*

I was still marveling at the Western array when Nick hurriedly entered the room and invited me to sit down. A short, high-energy, and finely dressed man with wild white hair, he seated himself in his high-backed executive chair behind a very large oak desk. Carefully placed lights above created a glow around him. Behind his desk, he had climbed a step onto a platform so he'd appeared taller and more imposing. I seated myself across from him, finding to my surprise that I was sinking deeply into a very soft chair, my eyes at the level of the top of his desk. It occurred to me that none of this was accidental. Clearly, Nick was in charge, and visitors were not.

I asked Nick why he thought his leaders needed training. With a serious, clipped tone, he told me that they were not following through on what he told them to do, and needed *listening* training. As I probed how such training might help, his face screwed up into a scowl, and he barked, "You're not listening either! What these people need is listening training." Noting that listening training was *likely not* the most important priority for this group, I realized that Nick was a very strong-armed, directive executive, in a compliance culture deeply embedded in an organization that had known no other style for over two decades. Training in listening skills, while possibly helpful, would never solve the problems Nick was describing. Listening was more likely Nick's issue! Improvement would require that Nick first change *himself*, so that new cultural norms could be nurtured. These folks were likely listening very closely, but also retaliating out of anger and fear! Trust and fear are mutually exclusive. If you want a respectful, nurturing, and productive relationship with others, you must first be the source of that respect.

Leaders *inherit* everything in their stewardship, unless they have built the company themselves. Entrusted with the legacy of others, they now must lead the next generations, not only as role models but as orchestrators, bringing people together to get things done. They must do so as the changes in the external environment force internal change. We are hard-wired to believe that learning from the past makes us stronger and more able to avoid past mistakes. In a changing world, this is simply not true. The truth is not here to fit into our pre-conceived notions based in our experience. It does not respond to efforts to control it. This chapter will examine the power of the culture, the formation of communities of practice, the power of conversation to surface truth and make things happen, the use of storytelling to convey intentions, and the need for respectful candor.

"Our moment-to-moment choices reveal and create who we are."

Leadership is more than "what we know"

Extraordinary leaders understand that leadership is much more than what we know. In fact, espousing leadership theory, belief and knowledge without consequent action is self-indulgent nonsense. "I will try to improve" is an excuse to fail, right from the beginning. Decide, then do! No "trying" allowed. Leaders recognize that the "symptoms" of life are a form of wealth to be acted on. The details of our days are actually the script for our careers, and even our lives. Our moment-to-moment choices reveal and create who we are. When we can see or sense when something is wrong, we have an opportunity to do something about it, learn and grow from the experience, and perhaps even accomplish something that matters. Unfortunately, leaders often choose to rely on "experts" to serve as the source of knowledge and direction. Clearly, those who have information and knowledge can be helpful, but without the experience and intuition of seasoned leaders, they cannot be the sole source of perspective and wisdom. Actually, organizations that retain large numbers of "experts" may actually have many "bystanders," and a bit of distrust is appropriate. True confidence, wisdom, and skill come from experience, from taking action, not from watching.

We cannot discover our purpose through thinking alone. Taking action requires that we feel internally the consequences of our actions. This is what teaches leaders that, no matter how dark things become, they can always take one more step in favor of the vision, and follow one more inspiration. Amateur leaders will ask: "how can I make the situation serve my needs?" The extraordinary leader asks a radically different question: "How can I meet the needs that are presented in my situation?" Again, this perspective favors action. It is a bit like making eggs for breakfast… you must act! Break the eggs, cook them, then eat. No trying here, just doing. Practice means action.

We misunderstand the power of culture

When undergoing significant changes in the organization, leaders eventually realize that sustaining changes over time requires focus on the *culture*. They often declare with certainty, "We must change the culture!" or "We must drive change in the culture!" Then, with ponderous wisdom and insight, they pronounce that "The culture will have strategy for lunch!" implying that past decisions and mistakes are the cause of who we are. It's ridiculous to criticize the past. The past brought us here and no amount of criticism will change that. When we blame our past decisions for what we lack today, we are attacking ourselves. Get over it! We did the best we could with what we had.

Unfortunately, these statements, and many like them, are only *partial* truths, sometimes totally wrong, and they suggest that the culture is somehow a problem to be solved. It is not. The culture is dynamic and a means to change, as the environment changes, and as leaders change the conversation. Amateur leaders like Nick hate unfinished business because it distracts, delays progress, and saps energy. They become impatient, declaring "Get it done!" These folks will likely do major damage to the organization. Such "high-testosterone" pontifications betray ignorance about how culture works, and mars the pontificators as arrogant, misinformed, or even naïve. The culture is usually not the problem, nor is it ever the solution! To understand the depth and complexity, start by accepting that there is no conflict between the old ways and the new. Respect the overlaps, their connections, and the necessary growth that has occurred over time.

"Organizational culture is a necessary source of wisdom, and is to be respected."

The culture of the organization is the context, the system of relationships that can be exercised to either support or obstruct change. The focus and direction of organizational culture are impossible to describe in our rational, logical, and factual language. Rather, they require stories, metaphors that reveal cultural truths from "around the edges," something not usually taught in the MBA curriculum. The culture is not something for leaders to arbitrarily transform, or otherwise bend to do their will. Culture helps us to understand what we are part of, but there is a dark side… when we are directed by *shoulds* and opinions formed years before that are no longer relevant. It is the cumulative result of years of experience, decisions, behavior patterns, expectations, rhythms, and rituals, all of which contribute to "the collective personality" of the organization. It is about connection: past to present, person to person, community to community.

It resides in the quality of relationships and emerges in the conversations people are having.

To be effective, cultural change must be a fermenting process, with ideas and energies percolating and bubbling through phases of living, dying, and rebirth. This is a messy, turbulent process, never simple. Organizational culture is a necessary source of wisdom, and is to be respected. If leaders want cultural change, they must change the conversation, relationships, and themselves. Such change requires a level of authenticity and a willingness to assume those responsibilities that will test and stretch even the most seasoned leaders. Responsible leadership honors the history, rituals, and values inherent in the current organization as the building blocks that have brought it to its current success. Extraordinary leaders treat the culture with respect and don't try to "out-smart" it or change it to something they prefer. That is just plain egocentric. "Too much intolerance or arrogance coupled with a constant focus on problem-solving can be depressing and, ultimately, disempowering" (Kotter & Hesskett, 1992, p. 149).

The culture of an organization is nothing if not powerful, especially in defining or defending itself. Extraordinary leaders trust that the culture will change as needed, once people change. With time and focus, the culture, like a personality, will *change itself* as these alignments take place. The culture is dynamic and responsive, and will change as a voluntary response to new conditions, intentions, opportunities, and challenges, responding to pull not push.

We are not "organizations," there really is no such thing

Extraordinary leaders recognize that business, commerce, and service are means to a better life, not an end themselves. The word "organization" is severely limited as a description of the enterprise, implying a great deal of structure, rigid process, and detailed methods for work. But all structures are unstable, fluid, and impermanent. Nothing remains the same for long. Lines and boxes, structural hierarchies, chains of command, and all the other implications of the word "organization" encourage people to hide behind their titles and roles, instead of taking personal responsibility for their work.

In the real world, people come together in naturally forming *communities* from many professions, interacting, learning, and accomplishing together. One of the greatest assets of community is the sheer diversity of thought. We are here in this life together to know, help, learn from, and love one another. Such community framework fosters curiosity, inquiry, play, and "deep dives" to learn and grow together. This is intensely more complex and flowing than the word "organization" implies. Communities of professionals are places to learn, share, and grow knowledge and capabilities, to serve customers and to serve one another. In a community, people organize *themselves* in many ways, including professional practice (medicine, marketing, human resources, finance, and production), geography, and functions. Such diverse communities of practice are themselves made up of smaller communities, each with their own rules, expectations, patterns of behavior, assumptions about how things work, and even languages. Much of what happens in a "community of practice" is less than organized, but more of a free flow of connection, interconnection, rapidly changing responsibility in an effort to accomplish purpose, and a lot of conversation designed to help one another understand what is going on. Very little of this could be described by an objective observer as "an organization." Actually, it looks a lot like dis-organization held together by heroics and established friendships. The good news is that, for the most part, it works. People help one another, they communicate well because they have the same language, and they generally understand what they are there to get done. The addition of friendship allows us to see more clearly through one another's eyes.

"We are here in this life together to know, help, learn from, and love one another."

Telling vs. conversation

Continuing to work with Nick, I learned that his decisional approaches reflected an autocratic style of leadership designed to establish and maintain control rather than a participative style—more "organization" than "community." Unlike participative approaches in which power, responsibility, and information flow freely, an autocratic style is based on the conviction that people are either unwilling or unable to self-manage, and need to be controlled. Struggling for control is about power, and you seldom find effective answers when you are struggling for power with another. Bradford and Cohen (p. 60) describe three fears that feed the autocratic conviction: "fear that subordinates will not really take the large perspective... concern that people might not operate as a mature, cohesive group... [and] the ability of people to operate with each other in ways that are direct, honest, and constructive." Nick was under the illusion that he needed to control, and was telling... not conversing. His highly "organized" world was going out of control, and generating an environment in which he felt he needed to "win" by making others wrong. Further, he had little use for those outside of his immediate operations, considering them ineffectual, including those like me from "outside." Leadership is not about conformity. It's an emphasis on exercising our unique perspective, talents, and skills to bring about changes. As Mark Nepo (p. 27) reminds us, "Without listening, we talk too much, and then wonder why we are not heard." Nick knew that he was not being heard, but failed to recognize that he was the cause of that.

Most of the people within Nick's domain described the environment as oppressive, demoralizing, and unforgiving. Nick frequently met questions with the biting challenge: "Do it, you get paid, don't you!" a response both threatening and insulting to those on the receiving end. People who feel that they have "lost" will eventually make the "winners" pay a price, and Nick was paying a price in the failure of his staff to do what was required.

Extraordinary leaders seldom if ever speak like this to staff. Instead, they see everything as useful, even resistance to their purpose. They appreciate it all as a source of authentic information that has both mindful and heartfelt content. Curiously, Nick thought the solution was training others to listen, as if they needed more information, particularly information from him. Nick made it clear to me and his staff that he considered participation, openness, and fostering a climate of helpfulness as weak and ineffective. After all it is *the leader's* job to *lead,* and everyone else's job to *do.*

Unlike Nick, extraordinary leaders come to problems and conflict willing to be influenced. Such willingness permits learning, suspends judgment, and offers opportunity to grow. Refusal to be influenced only hardens us, and eventually destroys us. Information can only affect us to the extent that we allow it. Eventually, Nick failed and his company failed, miserably, with Nick blaming everyone else for it. I wondered if the company's founder, whose portrait was replaced by the Duke's, would be proud… sadly, probably not.

"Extraordinary leaders come to problems and conflict willing to be influenced. Such willingness permits learning, suspends judgment, and offers opportunity to grow."

The art of storytelling

While Nick's story is dramatic, the harsh reality is that his "you get paid" attitude is more the norm than the exception in what we call "modern society." Leaders often treat culture and relationships as "soft stuff" (actually calling it that) and something to be manipulated, an arrogance that is self-defeating. Sustaining effective change over time requires participation and engagement, characteristics that cause people to feel pride, to willingly grow and develop themselves, and, ultimately, to take more responsibility because they want to. None of this is "soft stuff" and success requires conversation.

One of the most effective ways to cultivate such conversation lies in the art of storytelling, a powerful method for conveying, across generations, values, traditions, and expectations. Actually, the culture is established and sustained by the stories people tell. To effectively change the culture, the stories must change in our conversations. The script for any story is fairly straightforward. It can be told in one-to-three minutes and can be varied in many ways for interest. There are five key steps to any story: 1) What was the situation (opportunity/crisis)? 2) Who took ownership and why? 3) What was done to change things? 4) What obstacles were encountered, and how were they overcome? 5) What were the results, and what did we learn? This script, followed with energy, real names, and real situations, can be gripping, informing, and helpful to people trying to understand what is expected. When we tell stories about ourselves or others, we bring ideas to life and make our thoughts both tangible and actionable.

Leaders overestimate their ability to change others, and seldom recognize the power in changing themselves

Actually, change is a normal experience for human beings, who have been in a constant state of change since conception. Suggesting that people don't like change or are naturally resistant to change is common wisdom, but not correct. We have to be careful about what we "know," and understand that what we believe may not be actual knowledge but a rationalization for the failure of a change process and a way of abdicating responsibility for that failure. The problem isn't that people won't or can't change. What people resist is *being changed,* and, too often, leaders think they can and should change others. No mature adult wants someone else to come into their world and tell them who they must become, how they must behave, and how they will be measured if they don't. The right time to shift gears or let go is when you are ready... not when someone else decides for you.

All of that is controlling and dictatorial and produces resistance and some-times aggression. When facing a challenge, leaders are at risk of turning it into struggle, even warfare, "us against the world." We tend to get what we focus on. This is a struggle because leaders have somehow decided how life should be, instead of welcoming it as it is. This is fear, not inten-tion. Avoiding the truth in relationships creates distance and mistrust, and destroys interpersonal intimacy. Our legacy is never the projects and initiatives we accomplished, but rather how we caused people to feel.

On the other hand, when a crisis occurs or when something new and different must become part of the work to be successful, most people seem quite capable of changing themselves and their behavior. Every obstacle holds within it the opportunity to bring the very best to those affected. It is up to the leader to recognize and take that opportunity, and encourage others to rise to the challenge. Such experiences are "turning points," decisive moments, critical times when decisions are made and take hold. Sometimes, change requires a level of persistence and tenacity, time to learn a new competency or skill, and the resilience to overcome obstacle and failure. But those who are sufficiently *internally* motivated will willingly and rapidly change themselves. Change, as a leader, requires a change of heart, not just a change of mind or behavior. Without that, it is less than authentic, and will not sustain.

Change is easy to start, but difficult to finish. "Changers" view change very differently than those being changed. Changers, including leaders, break change into several logical steps: get started, go through a shakedown to work out the bugs, and move forward to standardize the process—a fairly rational sequence of steps. However, those who are being changed see this differently. William Bridges teaches us (Bridges, *Transitions*, 1980) that the change experience is first one of "endings, then transition, and then we can consider new beginnings." These two processes are different—one logical and rational, the other emotional. People tend to be impressed by knowledge, skill, rationality, and talent in others, but they are moved most powerfully by their own emotions, by heart.

> *"The problem isn't that people won't or can't change. What people resist is being changed, and, too often, leaders think they can and should change others."*

Unless leaders address both in their work, changes will likely be difficult, and perhaps fail.

Is the culture "ready" for change?

Efforts to transform the culture through "driving change," creating manipulative "burning platforms," and other power strategies for insisting that people behave in certain ways lead to resistance more often than alignment. Sometimes we must let go of what we want in order to have an even greater result! Conflict and emotional collisions occur for one reason—fear, and a desire to control. Even more positive approaches are difficult, particularly in a "problem-solving" culture that is always breaking things into pieces. Certain symptoms appear when cultural readiness for change is not there, and it is wise to heed those symptoms carefully: if there is an unreasonable faith in the power of reason over emotion, readiness is not there; if candor and respect are not present, but the environment is one of hostility or apathy, readiness is not there; if management has a history of broken promises, abuse, or retaliation, readiness is not there; if there is no expectation of personal accountability for action and results, readiness is not there; if there is an absence of shared and well-communicated goals and critical metrics, readiness is not there; if leaders have weak or no emotional competency, readiness is not there; if there is a sense that no one is in charge, readiness is not there. Whenever stress and anxiety begin to rule, the external pressures and distractions have hijacked inner purpose, and readiness is not there. It is hard to be rational when emotions have taken over. Heart and mind work often in opposing ways.

When strategies are not working, leaders are often tempted to change midstream to find "the one strategy" that will do the trick. Doing this repeatedly leads to a "whipsaw effect," often described as going from "ditch to ditch," moving from telling people what to do to involving them in the solution and then telling them some more. This back and forth can create confusion and dismay among employees, who wonder: *Do I get to think and have a voice? Or am I expected to just do what I am told?* Such confusion results in one long and endless breakdown, the opposite of transformation. Perhaps it is time to do something different: no more ditch to ditch; no more whipsaw. Sometimes, when life moves people into an anxious, even chaotic state, it is the job of leaders to recognize that chaos is a necessary step in transformation. Change is destabilizing, disturbing the peace. But without chaos, there is no rebirth. With respectful humility, accept the culture just as it is. Only then can you face the moment and take meaningful action. For the culture to be ready to change, the leader must change first, so that the culture will support efforts to get things done. Perhaps curiosity and humility are more powerful motivators than control!

Candor with respect

We sometimes feel that we live in an adversarial world. We do not unless we choose to make it so. Most people want all to win. Respectful candor is the platform that enables a community culture to adapt and align with the vision and intentions of leadership. Truth is not a competitive game... it is a team enterprise! We must rely on one another's perspectives. Thoreau tells us: "The question is not what you look at, but what you see" (from: H. D. Thoreau's journal of August 5, 1851). Sharing perspectives allows suspension of the quest for "more and faster," and begins fostering connection and understanding. Progress has become an addiction, and the cost is our authentic relationships and connection. Reviving that means conversation, active listening to one another's hearts as well as their heads, and taking time to share observations and intentions. Leaders know with certainty that among those present, all that is needed is already present. There is no doubt or hesitation. Everyone in our life has added value in some way... everyone.

"Leaders know with certainty that among those present, all that is needed is already present. There is no doubt or hesitation. Everyone in our life has added value in some way... everyone."

Truth-telling allows people to share their differing views, with both listening carefully—not to debate one another but to integrate the differing truths into a shared truth. This is important! How often do leaders come to the conversation with their minds already made up? How often do you listen for the purpose of argument and disagreement, rather than for learning? How often do you employ stories not for understanding but for persuasion, a subtle form of politics? This is all "verbal jousting," and such communication solves nothing when it is mistrustful. When people have reason to distrust, communication may make things worse, turning facts into "spin," amplifying hostility, and further confusing things. In an environment of candor with respect, none of these things will occur. If you judge simply on the basis of observed behavior, leaders tend to be a high-anxiety group, with many obsessions: overly detailed processes, rigid metrics, unforgiving deadlines, and countless meetings that accomplish little, except confirmation that there is too much going on. Stress and anxiety are forms of resistance to what we are experiencing. As such, they are great teachers, leading us toward those changes that are needed. Once truth-telling is established, however, the larger culture will move forward, supporting leader efforts in profound ways. The culture is not the problem, but failure to listen and lack of respectful candor, might be.

Several principles underlie cultural change

Leaders who want to change things get started now. They start today. There are principles that guide success over time, while respecting cultural values.

» Resolve never to begin to change "next week" or "later," or to add change to your "to-do" list. Do it now. Just begin, and make it who you are now.

» Great things happen when people come together in conversation. To change the culture, change the conversation—from results to relationships, metrics to values, strategy to intentions, managing to learning. When the conversation changes, the culture will respond.

» Never (I repeat, never) try to "drive" cultural change. You'll just do damage.

» Culture always pushes back. It must, this is a good thing, and teaches much.

» Take time for reflection as you make change. What is the culture teaching you?

» Let the culture guide your efforts to change. Be willing to be influenced and to begin by changing yourself! If you figure out *what* you need to happen, the *how* will reveal itself in good time.

» Have compassionate patience with yourself and those around you! This takes time. People must change their thoughts and habits, their relationship to the work and the people around them. This is not easy.

» Take time to truly connect with those around you every day. Work to understand how they are experiencing change. Change is emotional.

» Celebrate learning in the change process. There will be much learning.

» Look! Leadership will always be about attributes, values, skills, and relationships, and seldom about techniques or tasks.

» People want to know that they count, so ensure that they do. If you lose the hearts of the people who do the work, you lose everything. Define yourself as willing to learn and grow, as being willing to be influenced, and open to discovery.

» Thoughtful questions, not answers, help to surface wisdom. (Some examples include: What are your intentions? What is changing? What is confusing? What are we resisting? What needs attending? What

"Leaders who want to change things get started now."

3ning the Room

is the struggle? How are things working out? What is available to help? Who is available to help? What have you learned?)

Make peace with the culture, and make your forebears proud!

Enterprise culture has endured for many reasons, reinforced by the many choices and decisions of those who have gone before. Your ancestors and forebears have given you everything you have. Are you stepping up with a growth mindset, willing to learn, stretch, and build on their legacy? Are you building competencies for tomorrow's challenges? Are you behaving as if they are watching how you treat their legacy? Are you respecting theirs as you want your legacy to be respected by those who follow you? Or are you doing as Nick did, and replacing the portraits of courageous past leaders with the staged courage images of John Wayne?

Efforts to control the culture, the changes you seek, and the people involved will sabotage the success you are trying to achieve. The problem is that amateurs pretend they are growing and changing, but they really are not. And the extraordinary leaders around them can see it! The desire to control is your worst enemy. Successful leaders work with hope and possibility, a willingness to take responsibility and a willingness to act. They understand their role to be a cycle: watching in the moment, right now; teaching; asking what's next; and enabling others to act, putting the burden of control where it belongs, where the work is being done. If you really want creativity in the workplace, you must accept the mess that come with creating a new reality. The best leaders improvise, work with "the mess," face fear and anxiety, listen and learn, and take reasonable risks. They never complain about limits, but use them to improvise and shine. Ask yourself what you are doing to feed the culture. Nourishing is your most powerful strategy for creating dramatic and long-lasting change.

Two steps on the path to dealing with challenges and obstacles

"If you really want creativity in the workplace, you must accept the mess that come with creating a new reality."

Professional leaders must be prepared to nurture change while respecting the culture. Some approaches have been outlined in this chapter. Consider how the messages here apply to your leadership approach by answering the questions in Step 1, and by taking the challenges in Step 2. Take time to reflect, listen internally to what matters most to you, and journal what you are learning.

Step 1 (reflections):

» What are the stories that reveal your culture's values and norms? Success stories? Failure stories? Overcoming-big-challenges stories?

» What do the conversations in your organization say about your cultural norms/values? Name five norms.

» How can the current cultural values and norms help you make required changes?

» What two things can you do to feed/nourish the culture?

» What three things must you do to transform yourself?

» What three things can you do to deepen your learning, and the learning of your staff, so that the intentions of the organization are achieved?

Step 2 (challenges):

» Name one significant change that you want to implement... Why?

» Name three cultural beliefs and behaviors that must be protected. Which beliefs or behaviors must be changed?

» Make three small changes now to begin the larger changes needed to be successful.

» Define what others must do for this to be successful, and tell them.

» Write a story of someone you know who has accomplished a similar change. What did they do? What was the situation (opportunity/crisis)? Who took ownership, and why? What was done to change things? What obstacles were encountered, and how were they overcome? What were the results, and what did you learn? Tell this story ten times to ten different people. Make it a habit.

CHAPTER 11

Developing Others

"Before you are a leader, success is about growing yourself.
When you become a leader, success is about growing others."
— Jack Welch (Winning, 2005, p. 65)

KEY POINTS SUMMARY

» Developing others is not about teaching and testing!

» Learning is not about control!

» Eliminating troubling learning paradigms.

» Learning requires not only ability but willingness.

» Anything worth learning will focus on three things: breadth, depth, and application.

» You must insist on stretch.

» Sometimes, the best learning comes from differences and conflict!

» The extraordinary leader helps people succeed beyond their wildest dreams.

As suggested by Jack Welch in the quote at the top of this page, one of the most important duties of extraordinary leaders is the development and preparation of others to do the work of the organization, with the necessary knowledge, competencies, and skills to ensure high-level performance over time. Sometimes, what we call problems are the result of failure to draw on the strengths and talents of one another. In addition, leaders recognize that, eventually, they must replace themselves as well, so that the work of the organization continues after they leave. However, most leaders do not come into their leadership with in-depth knowledge about how to develop people. Rather, they learn "on the fly" through experience, mistakes, and the counsel of their mentors. Perhaps there is a better way to approach this.

Developing others is not about teaching and testing!

Phil was the production manager for an assembly operation, and had recently hired a new machine operator for the line. The new employee had some experience in other organizations, but was largely unfamiliar with the equipment in this plant. As a result, Phil assigned the employee to work with one of his best operators, instructing that the new employee be given thorough training on the equipment. Phil's instruction: "Just show him what to do." The training lasted two days, and the new employee was buried in an avalanche of technical information, different machine requirements, tips and shortcuts in production, safety information, and data about quality and productivity metrics and goals. However, there was no actual time spent on the machines. On completion, Phil met with the new employee and began quizzing him on the machines, work procedures, methods for stocking, process for maintenance on the machines, and literally every aspect of the machine performance. He also harshly criticized incorrect responses, failure to respond rapidly with knowledge, and the new employee's hesitancy to respond when he was uncertain. Phil made it clear that the new employee was failing in his answers and putting his new job in jeopardy, increasing the tension even further.

Later, the new employee asked others about Phil, what kind of boss he was, and whether he was reading the criticisms correctly, and the other employees reassured him that Phil did this with all new employees—it was his way of "testing" them. Apparently, this was Phil's way of making sure everyone knew who was in charge. And apparently no one appreciated it. They described Phil as a "bully boss" who destroys morale, puts new employees through hazing to see what they are capable of, etc. The new employee resigned the next day. Phil had to start all over in hiring the next new employee, grumbling that "there aren't any good candidates out there anymore!"

"As a leader, you are not in charge of the path people are on."

Look! There are no "mulligans" for these kinds of situations. You can't undo the wrong! What Phil did is expensive—and his responsibility! Leaders like Phil believe that their job is to tell their staff what to do, how to do it, when to do it, where to do it, and even why to do it—and then to test them . . . and that this approach was the proper way to develop staff to do their jobs well. Unfortunately, they do this because they want it done their way, for their purposes. They show little respect for individual work style, knowledge, or interests of the people who are doing the work. Such leaders foster dependency *on the leader*, rather than growing their staff to be independent, and interdependent on one another.

Learning is not about control!

As a leader, you are not in charge of the path people are on. The more you try to control people, manage events, and drive results, the sooner you find yourself frustrated and disappointed. When people feel controlled or "boxed in," their energy drains, satisfaction declines, and resentment and frustration build. Eventually, the amateur leader will voice concerns that nobody around them is functioning well. They waste resources for training and development because they believe their staff to be unskilled, while expressing extreme frustration that everyone around them is so incompetent. According to Michael Prokopeak, "lack of skills is not what holds people back" (Prokopeak, M., *Chief Learning Officer Magazine*: "Learner Know Thyself": October 2019, p. 4). The failure to build competence and confidence over time is the problem! This is a losing game! Training people with knowledge and skills without developing confidence, independence, and sustainability is not development. Sustainable change requires self-reliance and personal accountability.

It is not necessary to micro-manage to know what is going on. The extraordinary leader is present often, available when not actually present, and helpful when help is needed. Most people will do what is necessary on their own, given time, guidance, and support. Extraordinary leaders know the value of patience, and know that waiting is a fundamental skill in developing others and a rare skill among anxiety-driven leaders. They understand that developing others is much like gardening… tulips do not fall from the sky! The bulbs must be planted in the fall and then you wait through the winter for early spring, when the blossoms begin to bloom. This takes time… and so does human learning and growth.

Eliminating troubling learning paradigms

Leaders are mentors, coaches, and teachers. In those roles you must have some knowledge about learning itself. There are a number of self-defeating assumptions about how learning occurs that you must be alert to. A better understanding may help to clear the fog about how leaders can more effectively take on teaching roles.

1. *What you know affects your performance.* Maybe. But maybe not. For those who think that teaching and training are merely functions that impart knowledge from one brain to another, this idea makes sense. Our mind combines rational, logical thought with knowledge to help us navigate our world with some stability and security. However, practical evidence suggests that, often, this idea is untrue. For instance, in the area of safety, people are usually pretty well informed

about the safe practices and procedures required in their work. They know what to do and what not to do, and understand the consequences if they fail. Still, it is almost a matter of routine for people to compromise the processes and omit important steps in order to accelerate production for personal convenience. Then people get hurt, not because those doing the hurting didn't understand the rules, but because they didn't follow them. Knowing is not sufficient by itself to ensure performance. (Don't believe me? How religiously do you obey the speed limits? Do you text while driving? Do you wear your seatbelt whenever driving? Hmmm?)

2. *Learning happens in stages (building blocks).* The human lifecycle often works this way, from infancy to toddlerhood, toddlerhood to young childhood, young childhood to teenagerhood, and from teenagerhood to young adulthood. Each of these stages represents a necessary learning tollgate for entry into the next stage. However, this staged approach to learning does not apply to all learning. Sometimes learning is messy, disorganized, and even chaotic. The conducting of an experiment, the changing of a complex set of processes, or even the immersion of people into a totally new environment, with new challenges and new obligations, will create learning that is totally disorganized, and that appears incomprehensible when looking from the outside in. This is normal and natural. However, it's also uncomfortable! Mature adults normally seek to avoid or at least minimize that chaos, attempting to take a step-by-step, staged approach to learning. But this often fails, simply because the changes are too complex and inter-related to keep under complete control, and too fast to take the time necessary for a

"Extraordinary leaders know the value of patience, and know that waiting is a fundamental skill in developing others and a rare skill among anxiety-driven leaders."

staged learning process. As Mark Nepo reminds us, "being deliberate or methodical will not always help us negotiate life" (Nepo, *Exquisite Risk*, 2005, p. 106). In a world of constant change, you simply cannot control things and keep them the same, regardless of what you want.

3. *We can teach what we know.* Despite wishing that this idea was true, it's not. Not everyone is a teacher, capable of passing on knowledge and wisdom earned over many years and experiences. To be able to teach is both skill and a gift. Those without the gift seem to rely on the learning paradigm described in item number one above, and consider teaching to be a matter of transferring knowledge from one head to another. The true teacher understands that teaching, particularly with adults, is fundamentally a *learning* process, in which the student is pulling for knowledge and wisdom that are useful and applicable now. To the extent that the teacher can orchestrate learning around the natural "pull" dynamics of most adults, that teacher will be successful. Adults learn best in the experience of day-to-day work, when the need for knowledge and skill is most acutely felt.

4. *Learning can be parsed out into digestible pieces.* This paradigm is very similar to the staged learning paradigm in item number two above. However, instead of staging the learning process sequentially, the advocate of this approach attempts to break the knowledge, skill, and wisdom into smaller pieces—perhaps connected, perhaps not—so the student isn't faced with the prospect of learning too many things at once. There is some value to this approach, but only when what is being taught can be easily compartmentalized, and then later integrated in a meaningful way. Actually, this is what is done with medical students when they learn anatomy, physiology, biology, chemistry, and all of the other pieces that go into understanding the human creature for which they will eventually be caring. However, many complex situations cannot be treated this way. For example, strategy development, an important competency for executive and managerial success, is very complex. Not every question requires an answer, and not every problem a solution. Rather, we navigate the uncertainties. (For example: how do you decide whether to invest

millions in new technology or take that money into the establishment of a new enterprise in a new community? This is like choosing between apples and oranges, and there is no effective way to compare options. The complexities of cost, profit potential, demographics, history, cultural implications, etc., all serve to render rational approaches limited at best!) When considering changing strategies within a changing environment, with changing political pressures, and changing resource availability, absolutely nothing about strategic development is standing still. The learning process requires an approach that is fully integrated, as complex as that sounds. It will feel very chaotic, but with proper guidance and immersion, and the proper innate talents and abilities, the learner can learn strategic development over time.

"The true teacher understands that teaching, particularly with adults, is fundamentally a learning process."

5. *We can drive learning.* This word "drive" is always problematic, whether we're talking about driving change, learning, performance, or results. The word automatically generates a great deal of resistance in its use. (Do you really want to be "driven" by someone else's intentions?) When someone feels pushed, their natural inclination is to push back, with the net sum of this activity usually equaling zero, and both parties matching in force each other's push. You can attempt to drive learning, and many have. But you will, in the long run, fail. Examples? OSHA, EEOC, affirmative action, and many other compliance programs that have been implemented over the years with less-than-mediocre results.

6. *The evidence is in the metrics...if you can't/don't measure, it hasn't happened.* This particular paradigm is probably the most damaging, and the

most difficult to deal with, due to today's obsession with metrics. *Some things are immeasurable.* Despite our best efforts, there are very important things in leadership that simply defy measurement. How does one apply metrics to friendship, compassion, joy in the work? How about the exercise of knowledge, commitment, loyalty, and any other human attributes that describe the feelings and energies that people bring to the workplace? Such feelings in themselves are neither good nor bad. Their purpose is to bring focus to things that require attention. They are teachers, impelling growth. Sometimes, proxies for these metrics are used, like satisfaction/engagement surveys, but these are imperfect, incomplete, and do not address the full human spirit. Actually, these kinds of metrics are boring! At best, they offer a "finger in the wind," allowing a very general understanding of which way the wind is blowing. A more granular understanding is not possible, whether measuring at the group or individual level. To think otherwise is simply folly. It is the leader's job to ensure that learning is taking place every day in the work. But the goal is not learning. The goal is improving the enterprise in significant and measurable ways.

Learning requires not only ability but, more importantly, willingness

The old adage "When the student is ready, the teachers will appear" has profound implications for developing others. Extraordinary leaders understand that readiness to learn is required before attempting to teach anything. Learning cannot and should not be forced on anyone. Doing so is disrespectful! So, what is the leader to do if learning must occur? Amateur leaders tend to forget one basic rule of life: the best way to accomplish your desires is to help others accomplish theirs. Like Phil, they tend to kill the desire to learn and achieve through the imposition of methods, tools, and other vehicles for getting things done, rather than relying on the natural human imagination, curiosity, intention, and spirit. They then inject fear into the mix, with testing, comparisons, judgment, and other stress-creating behaviors. When judgment enters, it prevents any joy in the discovery aspects of learning. To judge another is to simply stop caring about them, and all learning stops.

Extraordinary leaders are not judges, but servants, helping others learn and grow to create success in their own lives. Life is an ebb and flow of people helping one another and learning from one another, an exchange, best taken freely. To the extent that learning can be attached to personal goal accomplishment, it will be a natural process, likely approached with energy and enthusiasm. Successful leaders view the world as abundant, not limited. And they assume that those around them have great intentions and a willingness to learn. As a result, they actually attract more abundance and support.

"Learning cannot and should not be forced on anyone. Doing so is disrespectful!"

Anything worth learning will focus on three things: breadth, depth, and application

Telling and unguided experience are not effective learning processes, and do not constitute effective development of others. To be effective requires more rigor and method anchored to how adults learn what they know and can do. Adults learn in a number of ways, including formal processes (classroom instruction, conferences, reading, etc.), mentoring by others who have already experienced and learned what is required for success, and practical application of the knowledge and skills involved. Most effective learning processes are comprised of a mix of all three approaches.

Still, that is insufficient for competency acquisition. In addition to all that, learning needs to focus on breadth, depth, and application of knowledge. Breadth means that what is being learned is understood in the larger context of the work. So, if there is a specific skill or body of knowledge required, breadth means helping the learner understand "the why" of the work, the purpose of the knowledge or skill it requires. A machine operator needs to understand the overall purposes of the machine, and what it is producing to contribute to a larger customer outcome, whether that be a product or service. Depth means being able to apply the knowledge and skill to the immediate work processes. If the machine is making a part for a vehicle, then depth of understanding requires that the operator understand how the specific part he is making on the machine fits into the larger product or service. This understanding enables the operator to detect flaws early in the production process. Application means practice over time. Thinking about taking action is not courage. Taking action is courage. Starting something, persisting, and finishing all take courage. For most skills, practice enables improvement in output with experience. In the case of our machine operator, how to best adjust machine settings to produce the best possible product in the most efficient way can only come with experience.

Developing future leaders works much the same way. Through formal, mentoring, and experiential learning, future leaders gain specific knowledge and skills that are required to master leadership. All of this takes time, practice, and proper guidance. This is where the giants come in. We all have giants in our experience, leaders we admire and are willing to follow, because of attributes they possess that we deem worthy of following. It is important in developing others that we help them identify the giants in their professions, and inspire them to learn from those giants what has made them successful. It is not possible to grow as a leader if you do not cultivate relationships of courage and care with other learning leaders. Doing so builds energy and willingness to change and grow, to be able to function with confidence and independence over time. When you commit to learning something new each day, you are rewiring your brain for growth.

You must insist on stretch

Personal growth requires that we do things that are difficult or challenging. It is about cultivating "stretch" in what we do. Many believe that, by providing insight, unmotivated people will be willing to change. Lifetimes of experience say otherwise (consider smoking cessation, obesity, political behaviors, etc.). People place unreasonable demands on this world. "Satisfy me, engage me, make me feel important, keep me safe, reward me, but don't expect me to take any risk or make any effort!" Often, people expect their work to bring them happiness/satisfaction. Actually, that's backward. Our growth is usually a product of painful experience, risk, or significant events of awareness. It seldom comes from cynicism, apathy, or safekeeping. It is up to people to bring happiness, energy, and joy to the work. In every case, the effective response to unreasonable expectations must begin with that one-word sentence: "No!" People can choose to learn or not, to grow or not, to survive or not, to surround themselves with people who have both the competency to do the work and the willingness to contribute or not. Roughly 85 percent of the population are natural followers, taking their cues from family, church, government, friends, coworkers, and others. (Source: Dr. David Hawkins, *Power vs. Force*). This is not self-determination or empowerment. Being told "no" to unrealistic expectations is not rejection. Failure to accept "no" is immaturity, and the consequences are self-inflicted.

"Personal growth requires that we do things that are difficult or challenging. It is about cultivating "stretch" in what we do."

Understanding that there are choices leads to clarity that begins with that simple word, "no." Leadership practice requires that you give yourself to a different way of thinking and working with others, one that combines rigor with intuition, insists on stretch, and encourages discovery and learning in the process of planning and doing. This is about excellence, not competence, in a competitive world, and it requires a vision for what is possible. Without a vision or heartfelt dreams, people are left with meaningless, often repetitive, tasks and actions that deplete spirit.

Too many leadership approaches dwell only on harmony and employee "satisfaction" in developing others. Such approaches neglect the necessary roles of challenge, discomfort, and chaos in forming a new reality. Breakthrough thinking means letting go of keeping things as they are. Not everyone comes to work ready and willing to stretch or be stretched. So why do we dance around this instead of telling the truth? We claim we are protecting others, but in reality we are protecting ourselves. There is always "too much to do"! But that is never the point. Are you doing what matters most? An extraordinary leader understands focus on what matters most and that it means entering a different state, disturbing the peace, and ensuring the people do not become complacent in a world requiring the continual learning of new skills. Growth requires that every day we stretch a little and do something new or better than we've done before.

Go and see!

During a recent seminar, I challenged executives to go back to their divisions and departments and walk around. I told them to listen and learn, with the expectation that this would provide insights about the day-to-day work. The exercise had an inherent trap, and all fell into it. They returned in a high-energy state, very talkative, and clearly proud of their accomplishments in the exercise, so I invited them to tell their stories. One at a time, each executive related what they'd found on their journeys, the problems they'd encountered, the waste they'd saw, and the difficulties they'd observed among their staff as the work was being done. But they didn't stop there. They also described the advice they gave their staff, the problems they solved for them, and the corrections they made in how the work was being done. They were proud, satisfied, and excited with this learning exercise! Except...

They all failed! Going into the workplace is not about the leader solving problems, making corrections, giving advice, or doing the work of their staff. It is about *listening and learning* so they can *help others solve their own problems.* Leadership is not about being the shining knight on the white horse swooping in and saving the day. Actually, when you do that, you disrupt learning and embarrass the people who are there to do the work in the first place. This is a form of shaming. It's disrespectful and not helpful.

From striving to meaning: make others successful beyond their wildest dream!

As leaders, your work is not meaningful unless you are helping others find meaning in their work. When you bring your solutions to their problems, you impose your will on others. This violates the human spirit and is disrespectful. It is your job to make *them* successful, and to cause them to feel pride in their accomplishment. How will your employees ever learn if someone else is continually telling them what they need to do, and badgering them when they don't? Your leader role is to be mentor, teacher, obstacle remover, and catalyst for reflection and learning, transferring your knowledge and wisdom into the hearts and minds of those around you. Learning and coaching are your rightful contributions to the work of the business, generating long-term sustainability and embedding competencies for the future. The measure of your success, your legacy, will not be in what you accumulate in the way of praise or things, but in what you share, give away and transfer, as you grow others to take your place. This is not something that's practiced in short bursts, after which you return to some "non-leader" state. You are a leader in every moment, every thought, and every action.

Sometimes, the best learning comes from differences and conflict!

I mentioned in the prologue that a lot has been written over the years about team approaches to getting things

"Leadership is not about being the shining knight on the white horse swooping in and saving the day. Actually, when you do that, you disrupt learning and embarrass the people who are there to do the work in the first place."

done. There is a fundamental assumption that, somehow, teamwork is better than working alone, and that it works best when goals are shared and aligned. Unfortunately, shared goals are an overstated reason for teamwork. In reality, the most effective teams are made up of people who like one another, regardless of felt shared goals. People must want to work together if there is to be a team. Further, harmony is seen as a desirable trait for an effective team, but harmony is deceptive. Because we are comfortable in a harmonious environment, we believe that disruption is in our way. It is not! Actually, the disruption might be teaching us something important. Kindness may be the most courageous thing we can offer during conflict and stress.

People very often want learning and change to take place, but it is the other person that must learn and change! This attitude creates dissonance, and a great deal of drama in the hallways and parking lot conversations. But when the team comes together, instead of addressing our concerns, we dance, and fail to articulate what the issues really are. Avoiding difficult conversation is not compassion or care, kindness or empathy. Disagreement left unresolved will turn into conflict, which is about power—never a good situation for a team. This is a disservice to the group, and it can be paralyzing, preventing accomplishment. Insisting on being right in our uncertain world is a sure strategy for being wrong! In reality, not much will occur in the way of learning in the team environment unless all come to the team with honesty about what is occurring, and a willingness to have their position influenced.

This requires humility and the willingness to listen and change yourself. Listening is not a communications strategy! It is about being present. If our conversation is rebuttal or defense, we are not listening, we are arguing. If we are simultaneously distracted by cellphones, pagers, and laptops, we are not listening. If we complete the sentences of others to move things along, we are not listening. If it is all mind and no heart, we are not listening. Listening, deep listening, happens in the gut, requires attention, and is never judging. Approaching change without such humility will only create defensiveness and will destroy any care team members have for one another. True humility is the path to authentic power. It requires you to have the courage to share with others what you fear will damage relationships on the team, and the courage to receive feedback about what damage you might risk causing. This is a clear signal that you care! The best teams cultivate presence, active listening, diverse thinking, differences in approach, and a priority on results over harmony.

"Listening is not a communications strategy! It is about being present."

Helping people succeed beyond their wildest dreams

Extraordinary leaders recognize that people want to be inspired, want to be given reasons for optimism, and will always work toward optimism rather than pessimism if given the choice. Contrary to a former colleague of mine, people are not sheep, waiting for a shepherd. Most want purpose, but rather than looking inside themselves, they are looking outside. Many do not realize that we can choose how we feel, and we can evoke more energy from within at any time. The extraordinary leader manages the thoughts of those that follow on meaningful purpose, and on the optimistic possibilities that present themselves. If you want extraordinary results, you must create extraordinary dreams and expectations.

Extraordinary leaders also know that people watch them closely, taking their cues from the leader's behaviors and optimism. If the leader displays pessimism, it is likely the employees also will. Optimism is equally contagious. Even more fundamentally, the extraordinary leader understands that learning takes place best when the focus is not on learning but on purpose. People will learn willingly and easily what they need and want to learn if it meets their felt needs and goals.

Two steps on the path to developing others

Professional leaders must be prepared to develop those who follow them, to ensure accomplishment and success that is sustainable over time. Approaches for this have been outlined in this chapter. Consider how the messages here apply to your leadership approach by answering the questions in Step 1 and taking the challenges in Step 2. Take time to reflect, listen internally to what matters most to you, and journal what you are learning as you do this.

Step 1 (reflections):

» Who are the giants you have learned from? Why? What specifically have you learned from each?

» How are others dependent on you? How did this happen? Can you foster more independent action on their part? How?

» How can you help people succeed beyond their wild dreams?

» How can you create an environment of learning, growth, and personal accountability for extraordinary results?

Step 2 (challenge):

» Identify three people ready to stretch into new responsibility.

» Assign each a new task or project that requires learning.

» Coach and follow up as needed... do not let them fail!

CHAPTER 12

Humility over Ego

"Those who are not busy integrating, are busy disintegrating.
We do not have the luxury of sitting still."
—*Mark Nepo,* Finding Inner Courage

⚷ KEY POINTS SUMMARY

» Leadership requires extraordinary humility.

» Many misunderstand leadership... it is not something that you
do, it is who you are.

» Leaders must face the unknown and unexpected challenges
with honesty.

» Self-mastery 101.

» Take time for self, to be alone. Reflect on and learn who you are as
a leader.

Do we celebrate our failures as enthusiastically as our successes? Do we define ourselves by our results or by the journey we're on? Does our dignity come from who we are or what we do? In a fast-paced environment, it is easy to become so anchored to successful tasks that we forget who we are— sometimes for moments and sometimes for much longer periods. It is time, in this discussion of leadership, to deal with ego, dignity, and humility. It is only with humility that leaders can break through the human barriers to change, the fear in trying something new and different.

I met Jodie as part of a retreat focused on personal self-mastery as a prime leadership competency. During such events, it is common practice to administer pre-work self-assessments to create data about personal leadership style. Jodie was an executive who carried her tall frame with grace and a very quiet charm. As we discussed the results of her assessments, I noticed in particular that she had profiled with an unusually strong "survival" orientation. When this occurs, it signals that the individual may be very concerned about safety, the fundamentals of getting through each day—an uncommon result for an executive. When I probed this, Jodie smiled, expressing a quiet surprise that the instruments pointed up this concern. Once assured that no one else would know what we discussed, she disclosed, again with quiet resolve, that she was terminally ill, would soon need bone-marrow transplantation, and that there was a very high probability she would die if the transplant was unsuccessful. This stunning disclosure put in relief for me the relative priority of things like spreadsheets, return on investment, day-to-day business metrics, and all of the other detail the leadership role takes for granted. This woman gracefully and calmly faced a challenge eclipsing all other interests. I offered her a chance to defer participation in the retreat until she felt better, but she said no, that she wanted to participate and learn more about leadership and herself. True to form, Jodie brought profound knowledge with a sense of calm unusual in these events, welcoming the retreat as an opportunity to learn and to disclose to her colleagues her difficult journey ahead. She also took the time to teach us all what courage really is.

It is a sign of courage and strength to acknowledge that leaders have things to learn. You cannot be an effective leader unless you are willing to accept all of the imperfections around you... including and especially your own. You never become a leader by changing the work or changing others. You become a leader by changing yourself. And you can't ask others to change themselves unless you are yourself willing to change. In leadership, everything is practice. To gain wisdom, there are a number of things you must do to grow and develop, to see the truth of your leadership. How you think, present yourself, and speak to others are who you are, and everything is practice. Reverse the common knowledge that limits your thinking and accept that answers create questions, solutions create problems, and followers create leaders. Immediate answers and solutions seldom occur, and every problem is an unfolding process. You must face unknown and unexpected challenges in the moment, cultivate the characteristics that will advance your growth, and regularly "go and see" what is going on where the work occurs.

"It is a sign of courage and strength to acknowledge that leaders have things to learn."

All of this requires extraordinary humility

Humility is not about replacing a sense of superiority with inferiority. Actually, this is a form of self-sabotage, with thoughts like: I don't deserve it, It's not fair, and I'm not good enough. Inferiority and superiority are both manifestations of fear. A simple test: Do you feel the need to be the best? To win? To be smart? Do you push yourself into the spotlight in front of others? Self-absorption and arrogance are poisonous to the spirit. They dull the senses and deeply damage life experience. None of this is humility. Such leaders are literally deciding not to listen and learn, and not to see the reality in front of them. Leaders who behave this way are striving for approval— and are destined to experience disapproval. No one likes being around those begging for approval. People who experience the most approval rarely seek it out.

To truly live humility means giving ourselves to work, love, and others, without fear or conditions. Humility means we are in alignment with our authentic selves. We not only know who we are (strengths and weaknesses), but we present ourselves that way. Humility is about living life as an equal. Just because we are maturing as leaders does not mean we have put our weaknesses and vulnerabilities behind us and can forget them. They are still there, and joined by new ones every day.

The very things that have brought you to success, if left unchallenged, will also undo you. Awareness of our own egoic self-interests is the most important agent for personal change. Real transformation requires a letting go of the ego in favor of truth-telling and transparency on both the rational and emotional levels. We want recognition on our terms, with full editorial control over the story: just read the resumes people write!

But recognition doesn't work that way in real life. Humility requires the whole story! Extraordinary leaders understand that it is dangerous to fall in love with our own sense of what is right, what is best, and what *should* be done about a whole host of problems they face every day. Rather, they learn to trust the experiences of those equals around them for advice and counsel that has merit. As Julia Cameron reflected (*Finding Water*, p.77): "The minute we identify with the rest of humankind, we are on the right track. The minute we set ourselves apart, we are in trouble." Our leadership practice is shaped not by our beliefs and striving for acclaim or approval, but by our actions and relationships that bring about value. Our human journey is an inside job, an exploration of unknown pathways that play out as we work and play with others. While others only see the external, our authentic power lies not outside ourselves, but within, and cannot be scripted. Humble leaders never compare themselves to others, but only to their own past progress. And as they learn, they become wiser in their approach than in the past.

Let's correct misunderstandings about leadership

New leaders are seldom imbued with profound knowledge and wisdom of the sort I experienced in Jodie. In fact, they often have serious and profound misunderstandings about what leaders are.

Who I am is what I do. We often treat our goals and intentions as if they have somehow come from God, rather than our own ambition. Being this obsessed is self-limiting and prevents the natural learning that comes from living life. No, you are not your job title, profession, or goals. You live, breathe, and work as an authentic individual, with relationships, emotions, and interests that go beyond your work. If you allow the urgencies and drumbeat demands of daily work to absorb your day, you will relinquish the experience of really living and experiencing your life.

Who I am is who I work for. No, you are not your department or your company. You are one person, making a unique contribution. If you think leadership is about imitating or pleasing some leader in your company, think again. It is likely that you are seeking attention and approval, and not learning leadership. Be yourself!

Who I am is what I have. No, what you have or do not have will never define you. If you are what you have, then when you don't have, you aren't. In fact, to get to where you want to go, you may often find that you must let go of what you have.

Who I am is what others think of me. No... others cannot define you. Who you are has absolutely nothing to do with any opinions held by anyone. Period, no exceptions. Never let your sense of who you are as a leader be conditioned by the opinions of others. When we put the

"The very things that have brought you to success, if left unchallenged, will also undo you."

opinions of others before our own, we are in an unhealthy state, and this will eventually lead to resentment.

I create my own destiny. No, not entirely. The egocentric belief that one creates their own destiny amplifies each of the other misunderstandings, making it difficult to see that leadership is none of this at all. Destiny is the result of both internal and external factors. Mastery occurs not in the use of force of will or control to achieve your ends, but in submission to the forces of life that challenge us to become more than we thought possible. Trying to control everything—the work, the people and the environment, is not leadership. It is just plain exhausting! Humility begins with a refusal to coerce or control, and then meeting life with acceptance and a willingness to listen.

Humility requires that you redefine how you think about your relationships. Do you bring to them your authentic self, with all your strengths and weaknesses? Are you being true to your own values, needs, and wants, regardless of other people's opinions? Or do you treat others as challenges to overcome, minds to change, ideas to sell, and people to "motivate" to do what you want done? Ego leads us to judge and categorize, as we figure out how everything works. Leaders routinely exercise such judgment hundreds of times every day, when meeting new people or having new experiences, to better understand what is going on. However, such judgments can work against you as you navigate your expectations.

Jodie, facing her life-threatening diagnosis, felt no need to judge or accept the judgments of others. She knew she was not her job, her executive title, the things she owned, or the judgments other people had of her. Any defining would have to be her own, and in that understanding, her leadership wisdom flowed. She had the courage to face her truth with honesty and a sense of possibility.

Leaders must face unknown and unexpected challenges with honesty

Humility requires honesty when facing issues and problems we have never before had to address. Some of the most challenging include:

The use of new power. Once you are a leader, others begin organizing around that leadership in an effort to support what needs to be done. People will then sometimes take a mere suggestion or the voicing of an idea by the leader as an instruction, and act on it, sometimes before the leader is prepared for action. New leaders need to become sensitized to the power of their words and intentions as they voice them with their colleagues.

The need to sometimes stand alone. Learning leadership occurs when you put yourself in situations that challenge you to lead. Leaders are expected to take positions on issues affecting the organization and the people in it, and often the leader's positions are in collision with those of others. Leaders must at times be willing to stand alone in their opinion, whether that is with colleagues, direct reports, or even those above, and accept that as normal. New leaders must expect such collisions, and learn how to navigate them effectively, keeping relationships intact.

Changing relationships. When assuming leadership, your relationships with your colleagues and coworkers change significantly. Some struggle with this, and make their own problems through denial or even opposition to it. Changes in power relationships often create difficulty. When you act to realize your intentions, you create tension and even elicit envy in relationships. The temptation is to forego your intentions to preserve old relationships. Don't! Leaders who believe they can still retain their old relationships within their new leadership roles soon

> *"Humility begins with a refusal to coerce or control, and then meeting life with acceptance and a willingness to listen."*

187

find they're no longer "one of the gang." In fact, if things don't go well, they may have to fire one of those former friends—unsettling for any leader.

Exerting your intentions. Taking on a leadership role requires that you articulate your intentions and then execute them with confidence and care as you work with the people around you. This is new territory for the new leader, who has previously focused on actualizing the intentions of past leaders. Be careful here! Never count on what you intend to happen to occur as you intend it. Leadership requires adaptability. Being intentional does not mean forcing or manipulating others to submit. When we do, we rob them of their own creative energy, making them dependent on us. There is a difference between force and strength. Force is the pressure, often too hard, to achieve a purpose. Strength is a deep-seated power from within, needing no force to pursue intention. Authentic leadership is not measured solely by what you have accomplished. Rather, it is *how* it is accomplished that defines the best leaders. Humility and compassion are siblings.

Managing personal anxiety. Endless change is seldom a lasting foundation for lasting improvement. Humans seem to be wired for beginnings, process, and endings, and stress seems to be a major and chronic complaint of many leaders today. A tidal wave of data about economics, world disorder, politics, and many other pressures feeds everyone's anxiety. In a high-tension environment, people pay close attention to the words, moods, and movements of their leaders, and tense up in the presence of negative leader energy, passing it on to others. The more intuitive read emotions quite well, so it is very important *for the leader* to exercise self-control in the display of emotion and anxiety. Because tension and stress have the effect of blocking clarity and sapping energy, their display is a luxury that leaders can't afford. Rather, they must show confidence in themselves and the competence of those around them if they intend to get the best performance and results. At their foundation, the effective leader understands that they must meet stress and anxiety with hope and gratitude. They know fear and gratitude can't co-exist.

Dealing with crisis. Every leader will at some point have to engage in serious, perhaps crisis-level, events. Self-doubt and fear are normal in these circumstances, but they will never lead to success. By definition, these events are unpredicted, often with little precedent. They're tests of the leader's ability to be noble, responsive, decisive, and supportive, both emotionally and rationally. Leadership will always be about such attributes and seldom about tools, techniques, or tasks. Failure to bring these attributes to the crisis will define any leader as weak and ineffective. In the chaos created by crisis, it is important to realize that slower is often faster. Take the time to reflect and think in the middle of chaos. Trust that as long as you take responsibility for getting yourself into your mess, you have the power to get yourself out of it.

Dealing with the strivings of others. Leaders work with other leaders. Many come into leadership with a great deal of striving energy, focused on not only intentions, metrics, goals, and results, but also a flurry of activities and engagements that generate in others a combination of adrenaline and fatigue that can only be described as distress. It is easy to get addicted to this way of work due to the high-energy cycles. Many managers have a strong preoccupation with tomorrow. This obsession depletes joy in today's accomplishment and erodes the spirit over time. We are never enough! In today's consumer mindset, if a little is good, more is better, and a lot is best. This is seldom true, especially for leaders. Addictions to data, speed, winning, power, control, approval, and perfection undermines leader success. No one can go full-bore non-stop without depleting energy at a profound level. Swenson (p. 42) asks, "How do you slow a careening world when the throttle is stuck wide open?" Such addiction is unhealthy for the leader and for those around them. People can and will sustain a high pace in short bursts. But as a normal way of doing business, a continually fast pace creates dissatisfaction and demoralization, depriving people of the things that bring value in life. By chasing adrenalin, leaders fail to take the time to listen,

"Trust that as long as you take responsibility for getting yourself into your mess, you have the power to get yourself out of it."

connect, and love. You cannot celebrate today if everything around you dwells on never having enough.

Dealing with mistakes. People make mistakes every day. We will make mistakes as leaders. Either we learn from those mistakes, treating them as learning events, or we feel guilt, shame, or remorse—all self-inflicted wounds. How you deal with that, whether the mistakes are yours or others', exemplifies how well you have mastered the disciplines of leadership. Do you view mistakes as normal, with acceptance and a spirit of collegiality? Or do you criticize and demean? Our leadership character reveals itself in those moments when we do not get what we want, when life demonstrates for us that, despite our intentions and sheer strength of will, she has other plans. Always treat frustration as a gift… as fuel for growth and achievement. Actually, mistakes are wonderfully rich opportunities for learning and accidental discovery.

Success is about not being afraid to make mistakes and to learn from them. Shame about mistakes is never a friend. It robs people of their dignity and sense of well-being and inflames a harsh view of work and life. Shaming is a cruel starvation of heart. The antidote is compassion, forgiveness, and finding opportunity in imperfection. Extraordinary leaders know how to forgive when things go wrong. Forgiveness resolves regret, remorse, and retribution, and opens the door to learning and growth. Effective leaders find ways to encourage openness and learning from mistakes made. Leaders must be honest and open about what has occurred, and what is being done to remedy the mistake. Such humility provides a role model, demonstrates openness and trust, and betrays a grace that serves to inspire.

Dealing with sabotage. Every leader will have to deal with somebody who clearly and visibly does not wish to be led. Such negativity separates people; intelligent, humble leadership brings people together. Such individuals are sometimes overt in their position, but more often covert, sabotaging the overall intentions of the leader, and must be addressed directly. They can choose to continue to misunderstand and be misunderstood, or they can take a breath and listen, reflect, and broaden their perspectives. Negativity is never a sign of intelligence, but a demonstration of refusal to take responsibility. Leaders must act swiftly to remove such individuals from the team, without apology or hesitation.

Dealing with self. Finally, leaders must take the time to reflect on and understand their own intentions, personality factors, strengths, and weaknesses. Every leader is the single largest contributor to their own difficulties and ineffectiveness. It is in knowing yourself, your gifts, and your deficits that you come to terms with who you really are as a leader. When we are feeling disturbed inside, it means that the universe is not cooperating with our perfect plan for how everything should work. We have two choices: change the universe or change ourselves. Reflect on both your rational and emotional processes, and value your own unique gifts and contributions. The rational brings reason and order to your thoughts and intentions, while the emotional brings in the more important human experiences that offer meaning and joy to your work and life. You will learn this from experience, conversation with others, and getting acquainted with who you really are.

"When we are feeling disturbed inside, it means that the universe is not cooperating with our perfect plan for how everything should work. We have two choices: change the universe or change ourselves."

Take time for self

Do these symptoms describe you or anyone you know?

» You are on an unending, obsessive treadmill of trying harder and moving faster.

» You experience too many surprises, collisions, and obstacles that you did not anticipate—and could or should have.

» You are looking for answers rather than reframing questions. When the answers are not self-evident, you speculate and second guess.

» You frame things as either/or, black/white, and right/wrong, increasing your frustration and adding to your obsessive energy.

» You believe that your work is terribly important and that urgency trumps everything else.

» Your people are losing focus over time (scope, bright shiny objects).

» You are experiencing increasing collisions between your work and that of other people in your organization, causing ill will and anxiety.

» You are losing emotional connection to the work, and failing to set limits and boundaries for yourself and your staff.

» You think it is you who must do everything.

» You fail to close the work with celebration before moving onto the next challenge.

If any of these symptoms describes you, it is time to pause and reflect. The price paid for the honor to lead can become very costly. In a "type A" world, it is easy to be seduced by the "need to achieve," and by the rewards that accrue to those who consistently go above and beyond the requirements of the moment. In today's world, speed is required or others might push you out of the way! You become addicted to success, and to achieving the benefits of success that you have established for yourself. The adrenaline rush that comes with meeting and then exceeding targets gives short-term pleasure, but over time, this can take a toll on health and overall well-being. You fail to notice that you are tired, irritable, and not much fun to be around. By the time you "flame out" in exhaustion, it's too late. Realize in moments like this that there are many things for which you cannot write a business plan. Leadership is emotional, not just rational. A failure to recognize your own emotional processes sets the stage for the treadmill, loss of energy, and the deepening sense of dissatisfaction that can cloud day-to-day work. True humility recognizes that it is time to look in the mirror and see yourself for what you are, and begin to rearrange who you are. Becoming an extraordinary leader is a journey of constant change, adaptation, humility, and even personal transformation.

Leaders often wrongly believe that, if they do the "right things," they can bring about successful, sustainable change. What must change first is what is going on within the leader who must change. So, what must happen? Here are some ideas: Take time to reflect and journal. Sort out the truly important from the nice to do. Never join a committee or task group without exiting another that is less important. Take some things off the to-do list and do them now. Know what you will say "yes" to, and what you will say "no" to. Know how you will decide. Make a decision to delegate some of your work to trusted colleagues, and don't look back. Set aside specific times for those priorities still on your list, and focus that scheduled time (*only* that scheduled time) on only those priorities. Get traction by getting some things done, no distractions allowed! Create a pattern of reflection, de-selection, and delegation whenever the obsessions take over, and make this the new pattern and the new behavior.

When symptoms begin accruing, it is time to create space in your life. People feel the most sapped when they have drifted from what matters. Humility requires time and a true intention to take care of self before all others, and failure to do so means that there is nothing left for others. Trust that if the circumstances around you do not feed your purpose, they will, with your resolve, eventually drop away. Your purpose and intention require that you not settle for less than you are as a leader. If you want your life to work, you must be present for it—now, in the moment, with humility that knows you have human limits.

Self-mastery 101

Ultimately, humble leadership is about mastering self, not about directing others. "True competence is more about

"People feel the most sapped when they have drifted from what matters."

growing in wisdom than accumulating mere knowledge. It entails striving toward a psychological and spiritual maturity that results in personal power" (Peck, p. 77). You cannot lead others well if you are incessantly chasing solutions and answers while failing to nourish yourself. Jodie taught me that there are more important things in life and work than "more and faster." Leaders must treasure the moments, be at peace with who they are (limits included), and face each day as a new journey, a new adventure. Brussert and Brussert teach that "moments of grace, epiphanies, and great insights are lost to us because we are in too much of a hurry to notice them. Slow down, or you'll miss the good stuff" (Brussert & Brussert, p. 53). Be clear about your intentions and proceed with confidence and authentic care. Be willing to call what is what is, no spin. And savor with gratitude those around you for their unique contributions to success. You have choices, and no need to seek out others for permission or approval for any of this. Do what matters. Being right or being kind? Possibility or fear? Security or risk? Wait for data to guide you or trust your intuition? Take credit or give credit? Create anxiety in others or foster peace? Offer criticism or praise and pride? The answers to these questions will guide you as you develop your leadership practice.

Two steps on the path to humility

Extraordinary leaders must understand their equality with those who follow them, to ensure success that is sustainable over time. Approaches for this have been outlined in this chapter. Consider how the messages here apply to your leadership by answering the questions in Step 1, and by taking the challenges in Step 2. Take time to reflect, listen internally to what matters most to you, and journal what you are learning as you do this.

Step 1 (reflections):

> » As a leader, are you managing or are you contributing? Controlling or enabling?

> » As a leader, are you teaching or are you telling?

> » As a leader, are you blaming or are you helping? Criticizing or praising?

» As a leader, are you creating good soldiers or are you causing people to be successful beyond their wildest dreams?

Step 2 (challenge):

» *Complete a personal plan for your own development.* Once done, "walk it around" with at least three people whose opinions you trust, and listen to their advice. Include: your purpose; your developmental history, feedback from others, and anything else that informs who you have been, your strengths and weaknesses, your desired future (target state), the competencies required to achieve your future, stretch assignments that will cause you to learn the competencies you need, mentors who can support your intentions, metrics and study processes that will be necessary to monitor your progress.

» *Choose a regular meeting that you usually attend and send someone you trust in your place.* Do so without reservation, giving that person the power to act for you.

» *Go into the workplace and listen and learn.* Follow these rules: No advice! No solutions! No corrections! Only questions that clarify and help you understand the work.

CHAPTER 13

Epilogue—The Profile of an Ideal Leader

"When the ruler knows his own heart, the people are simple and pure.
When he meddles with their lives, they become restless and disturbed."
—Tao, 58ᵗʰ verse in Dyer, 2007, p. 278)

"When we are no longer able to change a situation,
we are challenged to change ourselves."
—Viktor Frankl

⚿ KEY POINTS SUMMARY

» Patterns of extraordinary leaders.

» Complexity is a leadership fact of life.

» Intuition is a leadership tool… use it!

» The final test… have I built a community?

» To transform the organization, we must first transform ourselves, making space for personal growth and change.

I begin this chapter where I began the first. When all is written, our journey always seems to return us to the beginning. What began as a disguise, with an imposter inside, striving to prove that he can lead others, ends with something akin to naked truth. The imposter, now a leader, continues the journey. Perhaps, instead of a journey, becoming a leader is more like a quest, with an unknown destination, ambiguity, choosing risk over security, and overcoming unforeseen challenges and barriers. The important question has changed after so many years from "Can I lead?" to "Have I led well?"

The views in the previous pages are not the result of some explosive "aha!" moment but, rather, a slow building of awareness over more than five decades of professional work. The stories in this book are predominately stories of transformation—some successful and some not. Most described here have approached their work with the best of intentions and a great deal of energetic desire to make a difference—not only in their lives but in the lives of others. Most people approach their work this way, and are craving leadership that can unchain their potential, enable them to do what they are capable of doing, and provide a work environment in which they can satisfy their needs. There are always challenges and it is a complicated world. When you strive to improve the organization's performance and ultimately to provide what customers need and want, the tendency is to simplify, standardize, lean down, and increase the pressure on those doing the work to provide more output in their limited time on the job. Without heartfelt leadership, such patterns can lead to a very fatigued workforce, loss of energy and motivation, and, ultimately, results opposed to what you are trying to achieve. Much of management today is transactional. "You do this and I'll do that." Security is exchanged for money and work for time, with compliance—often grudging compliance—the result. Perhaps there is a different approach altogether. Showing up, completing tasks, doing the job, and managing and improving processes is insufficient, making people into reliable machines. Extraordinary leaders understand the tempos of life, when to speed up and seize opportunities, when to slow down and recharge, when things are favorable and when things are not. Bringing to work mindful intention, caring hopes and dreams for self and others, with purpose, passion and energy, feeds the human spirit. Such passion breeds passion, permits risk, and creates the willingness to endure. All of this requires that leaders step up and "own the room" within which they practice that leadership.

There are success patterns for successful leaders

Those who have never been leaders cannot easily understand what leaders do, how they do it, and how it feels to be a leader. Their views of leadership are formed by reports of parents and friends, a cynical media, and colleagues, who may or may not have had good experiences with their past leaders. They themselves may work for bosses who are obsessed with speed and productivity at the expense of everything else, preventing them from learning what a true leader really is. There are as many lists of effective leadership characteristics as there are consultants selling leadership training programs, all strikingly similar, with distinct patterns setting effective leaders apart from others. There are hundreds of characteristics and attributes describing the "ideal leader" and no one masters them all. However, certain characteristics emerge as a starting, but not complete, list of core competencies:

> » Effective leaders are clear about their intentions, yet open to the input of others. The best leaders do this without permission-seeking, and with a willingness to make the decisions required to succeed and a humility that allows them to adapt to strength, allow time for maturation, and learn from their experiences and those of others.

> » Highly effective leaders have a relentless focus on making things better for the customer, the employees, or other stakeholders.

"Those who have never been leaders cannot easily understand what leaders do, how they do it, and how it feels to be a leader."

» Highly effective leaders never mistake success for significance. They always focus on what matters most.

» Effective leaders tell the truth, without spin, and do not omit. They live in "the now." They also realize that there are others who will insist on turning truth into something else.

» Effective leaders build confidence, never destroy it. They respectfully insist that people be responsible for their own happiness and accomplishment.

» Effective leaders do not seek praise or blame, and take neither personally. They know that what others think of them is none of their business.

» Effective leaders inspire people to hope, to focus on the possible, and to rise beyond their own self expectations, employing not only reason but also emotional commitment to foster energy. They have the ability to inspire others to succeed and excel, proceeding with patience, encouragement, persistence, and clarity when things do not go as planned.

» Effective leaders refrain from judging others, and do not accept the judgments of others. They never blame and shame, considering such behavior unacceptable. Nor do they criticize themselves. They know that the "inner critic" is not a friend, and not a reliable source of feedback.

» Effective leaders share power, knowing that power given away can be kept at the same time. They enthusiastically seek out wisdom and advice outside of their own circles. Hierarchy means less, and relationships and cooperative spirit mean more. This is about inclusion, not exclusion.

» Effective leaders know that, often, being decisive is more important than being informed. They are willing to take calculated risk, and to use their intuitive capabilities in the absence of perfect data.

» Effective leaders take responsibility. They never *try*, they *do*, knowing that trying gets in the way of owning results. They accept personal accountability for their decisions, their work, and the results of that work. They are never victims.

» Effective leaders give up the presumption/pretense that they are always right. They know that people deserve a leader with whom they can respectfully disagree. They also know that just because they think something is true does not mean it *is* true!

» Effective leaders recognize that the word "No" is both a complete sentence and a decision. It is unambiguous, and must be used to be effective. Such leaders have the courage to decide: "I'm here, I'm real, I mean it… so deal with it." They accept that others will disagree, criticize, shame, and even demonize, but that such judgment has no real power.

» Effective leaders give credit when things go well, and take responsibility for changing things when they go south.

» Effective leaders never resolve to change "next week" or sometime later, or to put change on their "to do" task list. They just begin, decide, and change now.

These leadership characteristics seem to be universal across countless studies, reflecting the kind of characteristics most of us aspire to follow. People are willing to follow such leaders, to step out of their own comfort zones and make the changes necessary to improve their work. The journey of becoming an effective leader means sorting out those characteristics and attributes that are most in alignment with their natural gifts and strengths, as they practice leadership in their environment.

"Effective leaders share power, knowing that power given away can be kept at the same time. They enthusiastically seek out wisdom and advice outside of their own circles."

Complexity is a leadership fact of life

Complex situations and endeavors require thoughtful approaches. The capacity to deal with ambiguity, politics, innumerable collisions, and the many uncertainties of everyday work life is central to leader core purpose, requiring attention and the ability to be silent and serve. As John O'Leary tells us, "We may not control everything that happens to us, but we always control how we respond" (O'Leary, p. 12). Growth as a leader requires taking the time to reflect, learn, change, and experiment. Staff requires the same opportunities to reflect, learn, change, and experiment if they are to grow in their technical and clinical competencies. Transition and transformation are not particularly enjoyable for those involved, but constant transformation is necessary in a constantly changing world. It means letting go of who you are to become somebody new. Are you willing to be the creative architect of your own life? Your emotional side demands to know why that is necessary, and rational reasons don't cut it. Too often, people arrive in their professions thinking they have achieved "the end." They are "experts," and they stop learning, growing, and changing, atrophying the human spirit. When people stop learning, they begin declining. Paradoxically, most learners see the world as having unlimited possibility, while most experts recognize only a few. Yet none of it is permanent, none of it will last. In a changing world, learning is not optional. Anyone who keeps on learning and changing remains vital and more valuable, as their talents and competencies slowly improve over time.

Angela Duckworth describes "grit" as "resting on the expectation that our own efforts can improve our future... this has nothing to do with luck and everything to do with getting up again" (Duckworth, 2016). If, as leaders, we are going to have grit, let's be ruthless about respecting and cultivating all three practices in our leadership... mind, heart, and spirit. To exercise leadership from mind alone, without heart or spirit, is to forego our wonderful creative and caring energy, and the power that comes with it. The extraordinary leader uses the mind to service the purposes of the heart and spirit, and not the other way around. People who feel valuable feel energy and connection to the work. They achieve a balance that is internal, not externally fed. Failure to achieve balance means paying a steep price in the form of fear, anxiety, and obsessive addiction to things that really do not matter. You cannot achieve balance by trying to control your external environment. When we describe people as being "out of control," we really mean that we are failing to control them. Why do we want to? Rather, you must create an inner environment of peaceful support. People in balance seldom worry much.

As leaders, we get to use our intuition!

It is human intuition that allows us to decide with imperfect information. Yet many of the rational people among us struggle with accepting or valuing intuition because it is difficult to measure or prove. Intuition is real, anchored in a combination of experience, insight, and wisdom that usually is the result of years in application. Literally every executive, physician, and lawyer, and probably many other professionals, as well, will admit to their successful use of intuition to understand what is going on around them, and as a means of deciding on a behavior or action. Extraordinary leaders are no exception… intuition counts. They know that leadership often requires decisions in the moment, calling for not conformance to some rule or policy but the leader's unique perspectives, talents, and skills. Perhaps it emerges as a series of thoughtful questions or hunches that seek validation. Regardless of how it comes about, intuition takes the experienced leader much farther than facts alone can.

The final test: have I built a community?

There is a difference between a mob and a community. Mobs require conformance, use force to control behavior, are closed to outsiders, and motivate through fear. Communities are formed by individuals who willingly

> "When we describe people as being "out of control," we really mean that we are failing to control them. Why do we want to?"

connecting with one another, with freedom of choice. They are open to others and focus on possibility. In true communities, loving friendships can occur between people who are willing to allow one another to experience the world through their eyes and hearts. People who love what they are doing seldom experience fear or anxiety while doing it. Leaders who ask if they have a future in their world are expressing anxiety, and probably do not.

That question reveals a subtle assumption that their future is in the hands of others. They are not creating their own path! Those leaders who proceed with confidence are leading with trust. Trust in the intuitive strengths of the people around you, and in their willingness to do the right thing for the business and customer. When things go wrong, you must have it within you to repair the wrongs, and to learn and heal in the process. You must trust that, as your relationships become more open, caring, and aligned, you will learn and do better work together. When you allow yourself to see from perspectives other than your own, you are defining yourself as willing to learn and grow, to be influenced, and to discover new vision through layers of illusion. Finally, trust that, when things become chaotic and turbulent, you will learn, grow, and become better, more whole, not simply as individual performers but as communities of professionals working together for the interests of the customer. Success at this requires both humility and courage. Humility without courage is neediness, and courage without humility is dangerous.

Six steps to take now

So, as leaders, what can you do now to begin asserting effective leadership for your staff in the service of your customers and communities?

1. *Walk around.* How simple is that? Walking around with purpose and intention can be a highly productive affair. The idea is to spend time in the work and with the people who are doing it so they get to know who you are and you get to know who they are. In addition, you get to see how things are going and how things work. The more you understand how things work, the more you can be helpful in providing the

resources and advice needed for them to become successful. At first, walking around might raise a few eyebrows, especially if it's not common practice. It will take a little time for people to get used to you. But as that occurs, the flow of knowledge and communication will accelerate. And that is a good thing. Listen, observe, and learn.

2. *Ask questions without giving advice.* While walking around or when interacting with your colleagues and coworkers at any time of the day, whether it be meetings or interactions during breaks, asking questions shows interest. It also focuses the information you are receiving, helping you understand even more deeply what is happening in your workplace. When people feel you are truly interested in the work being done and their welfare, they share more and you will be able to help more. Ask more questions. The hard part of this is the "without giving advice" part. Zip your lip and learn.

3. *Be with your people now, enjoy them, and dream together about what is possible.* There is always and only now. Leaders are in the present; the past is finished and the future not yet created. The best leaders live and work only with those who inspire and dream with them. They never choose to work with those who create fear or carry fear within. When you are with your staff, it really is OK to be a dreamer. They need to know what you want to achieve, what your vision is, and what you consider most important. That helps them know how to help you, and most people understand that when you help your leaders, you get to shine, too. This is a powerful motivator. The most inspiring success occurs in businesses where relationships spread

"Humility without courage is neediness, and courage without humility is dangerous."

across departments and divisions, and where success is a product of people coming together in conversation. Where this is absent, there is inevitably much collision, misinformation, and blaming.

4. *Be clear about expectations and share information—a lot!* What you think and do impacts many others, both now and in the future. Leadership extends way beyond the moment and over current geography. We can experience life either consciously or unconsciously... our choice. Most people want direct honesty from their leaders. They want to know when they're doing well and when they're not. They want to know how you're going to measure their performance. They want to know what you expect of them from day to day and week to week. This is not something you can do once and be done. It needs to be a repetitive, regular part of your communication process with your staff. One of the most frequent criticisms employees have of their managers is that they do not communicate sufficiently what is expected, and what employees need to know or do to be successful. If you make this a regular practice, you will set the stage for success.

5. *Reward learning, particularly when it comes from failure.* You can learn from two groups of people: those who are doing better than you—take time with them; and those doing worse than you—help them. People want acknowledgment when they learn, to know that someone noticed, particularly their boss. "Individuals who possess [positive self-regard] are good at their jobs; they have the requisite skills. They enjoy their work; it satisfies their basic needs and motives. Finally, they are proud of their work" (Bennis & Nanus, p. 62). Acknowledging people is a validation that helps anchor learning and engagement for the longer term, and it's particularly important when learning is the result of a failed effort. When people fail, they know they have failed, raising anxiety that they have somehow failed and there will be negative consequences, even punishment. The leader who treats failure as learning will put those anxieties to rest rapidly, and cause a positive flow of knowledge, information, and goodwill. Learning from failure is learning.

6. *Finally, recognize that not everyone will want to go where you are going, and they might have to leave.* Understand that you will not satisfy everyone in your organization. That is OK, and not personal. Sometimes the best thing you can do as a leader is find ways for people who do not want to be in your organization to be successful somewhere else.

This is about transformation!

"If we spent as much energy trying to respond intelligently to the uncontrollable as we do to trying to manhandle it, we'd probably kick up a lot less dust and be a lot less saddle sore at the end of the day" (Levoy, Vital Signs, p. 180). Leadership is about transformation, both personal and organizational. It is a shifting of gears from focus on the uncontrollable to focus on the possibilities. We can either allow circumstances to dictate our path or we can create our own journey toward our intentions… our choice. It is not that your leadership processes are flawed and need repair. In many cases, your processes are obsolete and need total overhaul. This is not incremental! Designing your leadership style is a lifetime enterprise. Transforming the business means transformation of the people conducting the business, something people must do for themselves. Transformation requires of the individual not personal change so much, but a return to one's authentic, true self. It is only from this place that we can respond effectively and with energy. To enable such transformation, you need to change the conversation while you do business with one another. The old conversations no longer work, and will produce the outcomes they've always produced. As people transform themselves, the business will transform, too. It must, and has no choice. This is radical, requiring courage, tenacity, and a steadfast will. When the practices

"We can either allow circumstances to dictate our path or we can create our own journey toward our intentions… our choice."

207

of mind, heart, and spirit work together, everything moves to balance. Anxiety decreases in favor of excitement about what is possible.

Transformation does not come from reading a book, including this one, or by attending a seminar. Rather it is the result of active living in the moment. You cannot find your passion or destiny through thought. You must commit to experience. Action leads to passion, and passion leads to destiny. The energy you create or sense in others can either charge you or drain you. You choose what you will accept. The stories here, while all true, are the stories of others, on their journeys. You must take your own journey, create your own stories, and squeeze out of them the wisdom lessons that enrich your leadership practice. Create awareness, inspire others, make it happen, and deepen your learning every day. If you must briefly remove yourself from the barrage of demands, requests, and other distracting voices that keep you from tending to your own compass, do it. This means slowing down, or even withdrawing.

Leadership promises for a transformed environment (mine)

In leadership, everything is practice. How we present ourselves in any moment is who we are, as leaders. We are leaders in the moment. Everything in the past has led you to this moment, and this moment is now your opportunity to do great things. Honor the past, savor the future, but live in the now. Success as a leader will find you… there is no need to seek it out. Final judgment of your leadership ability does not belong to you but to those who choose to follow you. Pay attention to intention, every day and in all interactions, with focus on mind, heart, and spirit.

There is no simple way to describe or summarize all I've written here. To try to do so would be less than authentic and superficial. Leadership is a journey, and journeys do not finish with the final chapter of a book. In the end, this is about putting down the book, any book, and living your leadership in the daily work. The ideas and experiences written here cannot make you an extraordinary leader. Only applying them can! And that is up to you! We have much to do together. Let's do it with wisdom and care for those we touch. Let's make it more than business... a human experience. If we are creating our own leadership approach, why not create a masterpiece and become the masters of our profession!

Ending this is a struggle, because the stories and ideas within are personal and profound. Surfacing much of this has been, for me, an exploration of my own journey and my own failures and successes along the way. However, I will close with one more list, promises I have made in my various leadership roles. They are mine, and I take full responsibility for them. If they can help you form your own, so much the better. Have a great journey! This is likely the most difficult work of your life! Make sure you love it!

"You cannot find your passion or destiny through thought. You must commit to experience. Action leads to passion, and passion leads to destiny."

My promises (feel free to hang this, or your version, on your wall!)

1. Great things can happen when people come together in conversation. We will have many conversations.

2. To attract loyalty, I must be loyal. To attract energy, I must display energy. To attract accomplishment, I must accomplish. And to attract caring people, I must care!

3. I will never know everything I need to know. I will trust and rely on others.

4. I will build people's confidence, never destroy it. As a leader, I will strive to take everyone across the finish line. People want to be part of something great, and I will respect that.

5. I will never solve the problems of others for them. Rather, I will lift them up so they have the power to solve their own problems, with pride and energy.

6. I will tell the truth and never play politics with you. Anything less than that just confuses people and breeds distrust.

7. I will never accept the latest or greatest panaceas as solutions to our problem.

8. Leadership is not something I do. It is something I am. I will take responsibility, with gratitude and the humility that comes from knowing I am not perfect.

9. Leadership begins when we are first of all willing to change ourselves. I will change myself.

10. I know that we are emotional creatures, and feelings count. I will respect feelings.

11. I know that some will not align with the intentions and goals of the organization. I will respect that decision and the consequences.

12. I will keep my promises. I consider failure to do so as an act of violence to our relationship.

13. I will work very hard to ensure that those around me have what is needed to learn, grow, and realize their dreams.

Two steps on the path to mastering leadership

Consider how the messages here apply to your leadership approach by answering the questions in Step 1, and by taking the challenges in Step 2. Take time to reflect, listen internally to what matters most to you, and journal what you are learning as you do this.

Step 1 (reflections):

» Do you find yourself providing answers rather than asking questions? Why?

» What can you provide staff that will help them become successful beyond their wildest dreams?

» Are there some in your area who do not want to go where you are going? What are your plans for those individuals?

» What must you do to transform yourself so that your organization begins to transform?

» What is your "leadership manifesto," as a leader? What will you own? What do you refuse to accept? What is your purpose and your promise?

Step 2 (challenge): Schedule a meeting with your supervisory executive, and invite conversation on the following questions. Take notes, listen to wisdom, and begin building your plan for growth as a leader.

» What are the stories that make you aware of the culture, the intentions of the organization, and the status of your division/department?

» What is needed to place attention on intentions, both yours and your staff?

» What is needed to make it all happen?

» What is needed to deepen learning?

» How will you know that you are leading well?

"Leadership is not something I do. It is something I am."

GRATITUDES

We learn leadership, like many things, from one another, and from our experiences. Those who teach us loom as giants in our lives, allowing us to see from the height of their experiences and perspectives. There have been many giants in my life, too many to list here, but some stand out for teaching me their truths in ways that "got through" the filters of a brain that sometimes can be pretty hard-headed about things (or so I have been told!). I have much gratitude and respect for the foundational lessons of the "giants" who have gone before us, our "elders" who have taught us the basics of being human beings in a work/production environment.

Jim Raney inspired me to follow my inner voice above the noise of those around me. Jim clearly taught courage in his leadership. Abe Brickner was the first leader who "took a chance" on me, giving me my first real professional responsibility, though I was untested and ignorant in a lot of ways. Randy Phillips was the first manager who succeeded in pushing me far enough to muster the courage to resign out of anger and frustration, and then offered guidance to help me self-correct and mature my view of how things work. Ron Church (deceased) was the most "level" leader in my career, demonstrating total calm, no matter the crisis or urgency. Everyone needs a rock like that. Mike Speer taught me patience and perspective over more than 27 years of professional work, in three different organizations. He brought me a model of humility, something I do not always exemplify, and insights into my abilities that no one else could see. John Toussaint MD was an inspiring CEO, challenging co-author, and still is a friend. Of all my giants, John has manifested the largest, most ambitious vision, and the sharpest focus, showing all that what they never thought possible could in fact be realized. Dean Gruner MD is a healing giant, able to calm those around him with a simple smile, silly joke or riddle, and still deal with issues and concerns that are difficult, complex and emotionally troubling. Paul Macek has been a valued client and source of inspiration, "can do" energy, and a model of risk-taking in my professional life. And Dr. Susan Turney is a CEO model of heart in the leadership suite, an executive who cares.

And I am deeply thankful for my colleagues and friends who have helped me along with the writing of this book by being my informal readers and advisers. I bow with humility to Andrew Cox, Ed Hammen, Dr. Murali Narayana, Maria Van Laanen, Julie Brussow, Melissa Breen, Katie Ball, all of whom have offered significant friendship, counsel and advice during the writing of this book.

I offer a very special nod to Michelle Aderhold Volk, a natural teacher and wonderful friend, who patiently waded through multiple drafts with much needed and appreciated care, loving friendship and advice along the way. Thank you, Michelle, for your friendship!

And for my family, I am indebted to the mother of my childhood, who taught me self-reliance, and gifted me with some of her "hard-headedness" along the way. Even our differences were teachings that made me stronger. And for Debra... who has been my support and source of deep grounding in an often-confusing world.

And for all of the teachers whose stories I have told in this book, while I have kept you anonymous for my protection and for yours, I know who you are, and you have my gratitude for your lessons. Thank you all for your presence in my life and work, and your generosity in teaching me your wisdom.

READINGS

When writing a book like this one, an author must draw on not only his own wisdom, but on the wisdom of others who have gone before. The listing below is only a partial list of writings in which I have immersed myself over the years. All are worthy of an in-depth read, and all have helped form my thoughts, opinions, and conclusions. I have made every attempt in this writing to acknowledge sources for quotes and ideas, and apologize if I have been remiss in any way. These writings, in my opinion, are the foundational work for understanding and learning leadership. I have read them all. You would do well to read anything on this list.

Antony, J. & Gupta, S. (2019) "Top Ten Reasons for Process Improvement Failures." International Journal of Lean Six Sigma. March 4, 2019.

Bell, C. R. (1996). *Managers as Mentors*. San Francisco, CA: Barrett-Koehler.

Bennis, W. & Nanus, B. (1985). *Leaders: The Strategies for Taking Charge*. New York: Harper Perennial.

Blanchard, K. & Hersey, P. (1988). *Management and Organizational Behavior: Utilizing human resources*. New Jersey: Prentice Hall.

Block, P. (1993). *Stewardship: Choosing Service Over Self-Interest*. San Francisco, CA: Berrett-Koehler.

Block, P. (2009). *Community: The Structure of Belonging*. San Francisco, CA: Berrett-Koehler Publishers, Inc.

Bradford, D. L. & Cohen, A. R. (1998). *Power Up: Transforming Organizations through Shared Leadership*. New York, NY: John Wiley & Sons, Inc.

Bremer, M. & McKibben, B. (2011). *Escape the Improvement Trap: Five Ingredients Missing in Most Improvement Recipes*. New York, NY: CRC Press.

Bridges, W. (1980). *Transitions: Making Sense of Life's Changes*. Reading, MA: Perseus Books.

Brooks, R. & Goldstein, S. (2003). *The Power of Resilience: Achieving Balance, Confidence, and Personal Strength in Your Life*. New York, NY: McGraw Hill.

Brussat, F. & Brussat, M.A. (1996). *Spiritual Literacy: Reading the Sacred in Everyday Life*. New York, NY: Touchstone Press.

Cameron, J. (2006). *Finding Water: The Art of Perseverance*. New York, NY: Penguin Group.

Campbell, A. (2015). *Just Get On With It! A Caring, Compassionate KICK UP THE ASS!* Carlsbad, CA: Hay House.

Case, J. (1995). *Open Book Management*. New York, NY: HarperCollins.

Chopra, D. (2010). *The Soul of Leadership: Unlocking Your Potential for Greatness*. New York, NY: Harmony Books.

Clemmer Group. (2001). "Why most change programs and improvement initiatives fail". https://www.clemmergroup.com/articles/change-programs-improvement-initiatives-fail/

Collins, J. & Porras, J. (1994). *Built to Last*. New York: Harper Business.

Vance, M. & Deacon D. (1995). *Think Out of The Box*. Franklin Lakes, NJ: Career Press.

DeAngelis, B. (2015). *Soul Shifts: Transformative Wisdom for Creating a Life of Authentic Awakening, Emotional Freedom, and Practical Spirituality*. New York, NY: Hay House, Inc.

Drucker, P. (1980). *Managing in Turbulent Times*. New York: Harper Perennial.

Drucker, P. (1989). *The New Realities*. New York: Harper & Row.

Drucker, P. (2002). *The Effective Executive*. New York, NY: Harper Collins Publishers.

Duckworth, A. (2016). *Grit: The Power of Passion and Perseverance*. New York, NY: Scribner.

Dyer, W. (1998). *Wisdom of the Ages: A Modern Master Brings Eternal Truths into Everyday Life*. New York, NY: Harper Collins Publishers.

Dyer, W. (2006). *Inspiration: Your Ultimate Calling*. Carlsbad, CA: Hay House Inc.

Dyer, W. (2007). *Change Your Thoughts, Change Your Life*. New York, NY: Hay House, Inc..

Dyer, W. (2006). *Living an Inspired Life: Your Ultimate Calling*. Carlsbad, CA: Hay House.

Dyer, W. (2010). *The Power of Intention: Learning to Co-create Your World Your Way*. New York, NY: Hay House, Inc.

Eblin, S. (2009). *The Next Level: What insiders know about Executive Success*. Boston, MA: Davies-Black.

Feldman, D. C. & Arnold, H. J. (1983). *Managing Individual and Group Behavior in Organizations*. New York: McGraw-Hill.

Frankl, V. (1992). *Man's Search for Meaning (4th ed)*. Boston: Beacon Press.

Friedman, E. (1990). *Friedman's Fables*. New York: The Guilford Press.

Friedman, E. (2007). *A Failure of Nerve: Leadership in the Age of the Quick Fix*. New York, NY: Church Publishing, Inc.

Fritz, R. (1984). *The Path of Least Resistance*. New York: Fawcett Columbine.

Garfield, C. (1986). *Peak Performers: The new heroes of American business*. New York: Avon Publishers.

George, M., Rowlands, D., & Kastle, B. (2004). *What is Lean Six Sigma*. New York, NY: McGraw-Hill.

George, M. Rowlands, D., Price, M. & Maxey, J. (2005). *Lean Six Sigma Pocket Tool Book*. New York, NY: McGraw-Hill.

Gerard, R. & Toussaint, T. (2010). *On the Mend: Revolutionizing Healthcare to Save Lives and Transform the Industry.* Cambridge, MA: Lean Enterprise Institute.

Gross, T. S. (1991). *Positively Outrageous Service: The Ultimate Antidote for Today's Tough Times.* New York, NY: Warner Books.

Handy, C. (1994). *The Age of Paradox.* Boston, MA: Harvard Business School.

Hardy, B. (2018). *Will Power Doesn't Work.* New York, NY: Hachette Books.

Harford, T. (2016). *Messy: The Power of Disorder to Transform Our Lives.* New York, NY: Riverhead Books.

Harris, Sam (2014). *Waking Up: A Guide to Spirituality Without Religion.* New York, NY: Simon & Schuster.

Hersey, P. (1984). *The Situational Leader.* Escondido, CA: Center for Leadership Studies.

Hill, N. (1960). *Think and Grow Rich.* New York: Fawcett Crest.

Hitchcock, D. and Willard, M. (1995). *Why Teams Fail and What to do About It: Essential Tools for Anyone Implementing Self-Directed Teams.* Chicago, IL: Irwin Professional Publishing.

Isaacs, W. (1999). *Dialogue and the Art of thinking Together.* New York, NY: Currency.

Jekiel, C. M. (2011). *Lean Human Resources: Redesigning HR Processes for a Culture of Continuous Improvement.* New York, NY: Productivity Press.

Kanter, R. M. (1989). *When Giants Learn to Dance.* New York: Simon & Schuster.

Kaplan, R. S. & Norton, D. P. (1996). *The Balanced Scorecard: Translating Strategy into Action.* Boston, MA: Harvard Business Schools.

Katzenbach, J.R. & Smith, D. K. (1993). *The Wisdom of Teams: Creating the High-Performance Organization.* New York, NY: McKinsey & Co.

Kiel, F. (2015). *Return on Character.* Boston, MA: Harvard Business School Publishing.

Kohn A. (1993). *Punished by Rewards*. Boston, MA: Houghten Mifflin.

Kotter, J. P. & Heskett, J. L. (1992). *Corporate Culture and Performance*. New York, NY: The Free Press.

Kouzes, J. & Posner, B. (1995). *The Leadership Challenge*. San Francisco: Jossey-Bass.

Kouzes, J. & Posner, B. (1993). *Credibility*. San Francisco: Jossey-Bass.

Jaworski, J. (1998). *Synchronicity: the inner path of leadership*. San Francisco: Berrett-Koehler Publishers.

Lakhiani, V. (2016). *The Code of the Extraordinary Mind*. New York, NY: Rodale Press.

Latzko, W. J. & Saunders, D. M. (1995). *Four Days with Dr. Deming: A Strategy for Modern Methods of Management*. Reading, MA: Addison-Wesley.

Leider, R. J. (2004). *The Power of Purpose: Creating Meaning in your Life*. San Francisco, CA: Berrett-Koehler Publishers.

Mainiaro, L. A. & Tromley, C. L. (1994). *Developing Managerial Skills in Organizational Behavior*. Englewood Cliffs, NJ: Prentice Hall.

Maldonado, M. (2014). "Leading with Excellence: Mindful Leadership Training and Exceptional Organizations": Human Capital Insights, Performance Management. March 2014.

Maltz, M. (1960). *Psycho-Cybernetics*. N. Hollywood, CA: Wilshire Books.

Maurer, R. (1996). *Beyond the Wall of Resistance*. Austin, TX: Bard Books, Incorporated.

Mazlow, A. (1943). "A Theory of Human Motivation". *Psychological Review*, 50, 370-396.

Moore, T. (2017). *Ageless Soul: the lifelong journey toward meaning and joy*. New York, NY: St. Martin's Press.

Myss, PhD, C. (1996). *Anatomy of the Spirit*. New York, NY: Three Rivers Press.

Nelson, M. C. (2008). *How We Lead Matters: Reflections on a Life of Leadership*. New York, NY: McGraw-Hill.

Nepo, M. (2005). *The Exquisite Risk: Daring to Live an Authentic Life*. New York, NY: Three Rivers Press.

Nepo, M. (2007). *Finding Inner Courage*. San Francisco, CA: Consari Press.

Orloff MD, Judith (2004). *Positive Energy: 10 Extraordinary Prescriptions for Transforming Fatigue, Stress & Fear into Vibrance, Strength & Love*. New York, NY: Three Rivers Press.

Orloff MD, Judith (2009). *Emotional Freedom*. New York, NY: Three Rivers Press.

Pande, P.E., Neuman, R. P. & Cavanagh, R.R. (2000). *The Six Sigma Way*. New York, NY: McGraw-Hill.

Peck, M. S. (1987). *The Different Drum: Community Making and Peace*. New York: Touchstone Books.

Peck, M. S. (1997). *The Road Less Traveled & Beyond*. New York, NY: Simon & Schuster.

Peters, T. (1987). *Thriving on Chaos*. New York, NY: Alfred A. Knopf.

Pressfield, Steven (2011). *Do the Work*. Do You Zoom, Inc. Amazon.com.

Rassouli (2016). *The Book of Creativity: Mastering your Creative Power*. Victoria, Australia 3150: Blue Angel Publishing.

Robbins, H.A. and Finley, M. (2000). *The New Why Teams Don't Work: What goes wrong and how to make it right*. San Francisco, CA: Barrett-Kohler Publishers.

Rubrich, L. (2004). *How to Prevent Lean Implementation Failures: 10 Reasons Why Failures Occur*. Ft. Wayne, IN: WCM Associates.

Ruiz, D. M. (2000). *The Four Agreements: Companions Book* San Rafael, CA: Amber-Allen Publishing, Inc.

Ryan, K. & Oestreich, D. (1991). *Driving Fear out of the Workplace*. San Francisco: Jossey-Bass.

Schaef, A.W. (1990) *Meditations for Women*. New York, NY. Harper-Collins.

Senge, P. (1990). *The Fifth Discipline*. New York: Doubleday.

Senge, P., Roberts, C., Ross, R., Smith, B., & Kleine, A. (1994). *The Fifth Discipline Field Book*. New York: Doubleday.

Senge, P., Scharmer, C.O., Jaworski, J., Flowers, B.S. (2004). *Presence: An Exploration of Profound Change in People, Organizations, and Society*. New York, NY: Doubleday.

Sewell, C. & Brown, P. (1990). *Customers for Life: How to Turn That One-Time Buyer into a Lifetime Customer*. New York, NY: Pocket Books.

Shook, J. (2008). *Managing to Learn: Using the A3 Management Process to Solve Problems, Gain Agreement, Mentor and Lead*. Cambridge, MA: The Lean Enterprise Institute.

Shtogren, J. A. (1980). *Models for Management: The Structure of Competence*. Woodlands, TX: Teleometrics International.

Singer, M. A. (2017). *The Untethered Soul: the Journey Beyond Yourself*. Oakland, CA: New Harbinger Publications and Noetic Books.

Sisk, H. L. & Williams, J. C. (1981). *Management & Organization*. Cincinnati, OH: Southwest Publishing Company.

Sobek, D. K. & Smalley, A. (2008). *Understanding A3 Thinking*. New York, NY: CRC Press.

Sonnenberg, F. (2012). "The Destructive Force of Fear". Frank Sonnenberg Online: https://www.franksonnenbergonline.com/leadership/the-only-thing-we-have-to-fear-is-fear-itself/

Starr, P. (1982). *The Social Transformation of American Medicine*. New York: Basic Books, Incorporated.

Steinmetz, L. L. & Todd, H. R. Jr. (1983). *First-Line Management*. Plano, TX: Business Publications, Inc.

Swenson, R.A. (2004). *Margin: Restoring Emotional, Physical, Financial and Time Reserves to Overloaded Lives*. Colorado Springs, CO: NavPress.

Tolle, E. (1999). *The Power of Now*. Novato, CA: Hamaste Publishing.

Waterman, R. H. (1987). *The Renewal Factor*. New York: Bantam Books.

Wheatley, M. J. (1992). *Leadership and the New Science*. San Francisco: Barrett-Koehler.

Woodcock, M. & Francis, D. (1979). *Unblocking Your Organization*. San Diego, CA: University Associates.

Zukav, G. (2000). *Soul Stories*. New York, NY: Simon & Schuster.

Zukav, G. (2014). *The Seat of the Soul*. New York, NY: Simon & Schuster.

ABOUT THE AUTHOR

 Dr. Roger Gerard is the owner of Sloan & Gerard Consulting, a private consulting practice serving executives and boards in strategic planning, operational planning, executive coaching, and management development. He also specializes in process improvement, and the use of lean methodologies in bringing about significant and measurable organizational improvement. He is the former Chief Learning Officer for ThedaCare, a N. E. Wisconsin-based integrated healthcare delivery system, retiring from that position in 2014. Roger has a 48-year career history that includes primarily significant work within the healthcare industry. However, he has also spent a quarter of his career in manufacturing and service industries nationwide. In addition, he has his own creative photography/illustration business that he shares with his wife, Debra.

Prior to his 23-year tenure with ThedaCare, Roger served as Vice President of Northern Michigan Hospitals in Petoskey, Michigan (1990-1991), and as the Director of Organizational Development (1985-1990). Before joining NMH, Roger was Creative Manager for Quality Systems for Sandy Corporation in Troy, Michigan, one of the largest training/consulting firms in the Midwest. With Sandy, he consulted with major clients (Burroughs, IBM, General Motors, Hyatt, etc.) on systemic leadership development and quality improvement projects. He also spent three years as Management Development Specialist for Gulf + Western Manufacturing, a Fortune 100 company.

Roger has over 40 years of experience leading executive and management development initiatives, in both large and small organization environments, focusing specifically on organizational performance improvement processes. He has co-authored a book published through the Lean Enterprise Institute entitled "On the Mend" focused on the ThedaCare Lean Journey, and has presented at numerous national conferences and locally throughout Wisconsin and Michigan on lean in the healthcare industry, and once served as Chair of the HealthCare Track at the Association for Manufacturing Excellence (AME) in Dallas. Roger is a member of ASQ, SHRM and OD Network. He earned his Ph.D. in Management and Applied Decision Sciences from Walden University in 2001.

Dr. Gerard is married to Debra, and has three adult daughters and one son, and among them six grandchildren.

Readers can reach Roger at: https//www.sloangerard.com

CPSIA information can be obtained
at www.ICGtesting.com
Printed in the USA
LVHW091311271020
669945LV00008B/375